M000203429

My Journey Through Four Worlds

Growing Up in the Japanese, Deaf, Hearing, and American Worlds

RONALD M. HIRANO

First Edition, 2021

Published by Savory Words Publishing
www.savorywords.com

© 2021

All rights reserved under international copyright conventions.
No part of this publication may be reproduced or transmitted in
any form or by other means, electronic or mechanical, including
photocopying, recording, or any other information storage and
retrieval system, without the written permission of the publisher,
except in the case of brief quotations or excerpts embodied in
critical articles or reviews.

ISBN 978-1-7377117-0-4
Printed in the United States of America

DEDICATION

*For the siblings, children, grandchildren, and relatives of
James Shigeo and Mary Shizue Hirano*

In memory of James and Mary

Japanese Clan Crest

TABLE OF CONTENTS

PREFACE

The human brain does not discriminate between the hands and the tongue. People discriminate.

— Dr. Laura Ann Pettito

In this book, each moment of writing has captured memorables time in my life. My life has been embodied by observant, immersive, ingenious and perseverant traits. When I was a child, one Sunday morning, my mother Mary compelled me to sing in a church choir. I indignantly clammed up. That incident made me resentful toward her, and it also created my lifelong aversion to oralism.

Undeterred, my mother urged me to learn speech and lipreading. I reacted strongly, and I pointed to my mouth and then my head. In brief, my lips represented oralism and my head or brain represented education. I asked her which one would be essential, and she left me alone after that. Up to this day, I communicate using American Sign Language (ASL) and easily resort to pencil and pad, gestures, and mobile text-voice conversion apps to communicate with non-signers.

During the late nineteenth century and the early twentieth century, migrants from Japan faced intolerance in the United States. They were exploited for decades, but they eventually overcame obstacles to liberty, success and prosperity in agriculture, business, industry and politics. Likewise, Deaf people suffered from authoritarianism and audism in education, culture, and employment for centuries, even today.

We have long struggled for equality and rights. Although we have surmounted barriers and reached our ultimate goals of independence and enlightenment, there remains much to be done in many areas. One such area is Deaf *Nikkei* — Americans of Japanese ancestry or Japanese-Americans in general.

Hearing white people and deaf oralists have not and do not recognize Nikkei ethnicity and Deaf culture. Hence, Nikkei and Deaf people have long experienced prejudice as a result of this lack of insight and rationality among supremacists and amoral advocates of speech and lip-reading. This book strives to preserve the virtue of ASL and Deaf culture and to enhance that way for public community.

Fortitude and serenity have reflected upon Deaf Nikkei like me, and shaped my upbringing and perspectives.

Disclaimer: I wrote this book to the best of my recollection.

FOREWORD

At a luncheon with my brother Ronnie, he asked if I would write a foreword to his autobiography, which he has dedicated ceaseless hours to especially in researching and writing. As the oldest of six children in our family, Ronnie has always been a shining example of hard work and sacrifice, no matter what task he sets out to accomplish. The word "cannot" was never a part of Ronnie's vocabulary, his being Deaf never an excuse not to face challenges that life presented to him. So really, how could I dare deny my brother this request?

In the process of writing this book, Ronnie was sadly discouraged by some members of our family and me, partly because we wanted to protect him. Would such an effort be misunderstood and seen only as narcissistic? Would some of the examples he shared involving members of our family or even close friends be received with distaste, even anger, perhaps causing schisms of misunderstanding? Would some harshly criticize him for not protecting their privacy and wash their hands of him? I was surprised with his response to our feedback, when he stopped writing for a while as he quietly mulled over his disappointment at our responses. As a younger man, he would have quickly exploded in anger, his quick deft fingers firing off words of anguish to us. But no, he was amazingly calm and reflective, fully understanding why we held these perspectives: we were so protective of him. However, after many months of deep thought and inactivity, he announced to family and friends that he would continue this autobiography. He had a story he was compelled to share.

I believe that my brother's autobiography is unique. He was the first-born Japanese-American Deaf child of James and Mary Hirano, both hearing. My second brother, Robert (Bobby), born eighteen months later, was hard of hearing. I know that my parents often were asked about the medical reasons for their sons' disabilities, but a doctor advised them to see Delight Rice, a hearing daughter of Deaf parents, for consultation. For as long as I know, I have heard my parents use the Japanese phrase, *Shi-ga-ta nai*, or "It cannot be helped." It became a mantra that carried them through the thick and thin of their lives, helping them deal with events beyond their control. My parents, being of immigrant stock with such strength and resolve, did not choose to be stuck with guilt and remorse over their sons' conditions; instead, they moved on as best as they could to provide a happy, secure home.

My brothers created their own sign language and could easily communicate with each other early on. Many family members regret that they did not record the boys' language, which demonstrated how inventive and creative the boys could be. To me, my brothers demonstrated that anything is possible when you want to communicate with another person, especially a brother.

Our life as a family on California Street in Berkeley was idyllic with Ronnie settling in happily as a student at the nearby California School for the Deaf. A very social child, Ronnie made friends with such ease. His wide smile and positive attitude were like magnets, winning the favor of his peers as well as the school staff. Being one of the few Asian Deaf students in attendance, attention and curiosity easily drifted Ronnie's way. Each day, he could not wait to go to school where he could communicate with ease, his swift and capable fingers forming letters and signs that those around him read and understood. Ronnie told me many years later that it was rare for a family with a Deaf child to master sign language, so for many Deaf children, home was the loneliest place. When I picture Ronnie at home with us, his head was always deeply buried in a book even at dinnertime, isolated from the rich conversations the rest of us had in spoken English and Japanese. It is no coincidence that he became an avid reader, hungrily swallowing up information that the written word brought him. As an adult, Ronnie served as the editor of newsletters and an author because he had learned firsthand the significance of reading and research information that brought life and breath to his writing.

When Ronnie was six years old, I was born as the third child and as a daughter who was hearing. It was not more than three years afterwards that the United States engaged in World War II with Japan. Our family and some 120,000 Japanese-Americans along the west coast, under Executive Order 9066 issued by President Franklin D. Roosevelt, were removed from our homes and sent to relocation camps in western and southern regions of the country, the government fearful of espionage. My parents were in a tailspin as they prepared for this evacuation, packing only what they could carry as ordered. Paramount in my mother's mind was nine-year-old Ronnie, knowing that education for her son in an internment camp would be greatly inadequate. Despite protests from the family, mainly my father and fraternal grandmother, our mother stood steadfast and decided that Ronnie could not and would not go to the Topaz relocation camp in Utah.

Miraculously, it was Delight Rice who offered to care for Ronnie in her home in Berkeley during this period of incarceration. Even as I write this, I am overwhelmed with emotion as I think of Delight, who believed in my brother so strongly that she took it upon herself to become his guardian while we were away. And then, picture if you will, a nine-year-old Japanese-American boy with downcast eyes standing beside a tall white lady at a boarding stop as hundreds of Japanese-Americans were climbing into buses traveling to Tanforan Assembly Camp, a San Bruno racetrack where the internees would stay until relocation camps were ready, bidding farewell to his family. For years, it was this particular scene at the bus stop that our mother repeatedly described, haunted by leaving Ronnie behind in Berkeley.

Long after all my siblings were married and had left home, my mother, knowing that we would have Ronnie and his wife Kay for Thanksgiving dinner in a few days, requested that I share how guilty she felt about not taking him to Topaz with us. Ron, without any hesitation, waved his hands saying, "No, no, Mom shouldn't feel that way." He said that it was a wonderful experience living with Delight, who opened his eyes to the ways of the world and who communicated daily to him in sign language, even interpreting the Lone Ranger radio series to him. She was the one who taught him how to save money, opening up a bank account for him. How fortunate he was to have his life so textured and rich so that he could stand tall and confident today and share his stories with you.

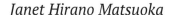

Janet Hirano Matsuoka

INTRODUCTION

Ronald Masato Hirano is ten years older than me, and at ten years old he was separated from our family. Ronnie was not with our family incarcerated in the Topaz Relocation Camp, where I was born. He was not with us when we returned to San Francisco's Japantown in 1945. It was only when our family moved to Berkeley in 1953 that he finally rejoined our family. From that period on, I was aware of Ronnie as my older brother, but I recall very little of the few daily contacts I had with him. I attribute this to his being a teen, wanting nothing to do with others, especially family members. But even when I try to describe my experience with Ronnie from then on, I draw a blank. Of course, there were the countless times Gordie, our younger brother, and I passed through the bedroom that Ronnie shared with another brother, Bobby, without acknowledging him. I remember attending Ronnie and Kay's wedding in Milwaukee but not much more. Regretfully, I now realize how very little I knew about my brother.

Nobody in our family signed except Bobby. In truth, I'm not entirely sure how our mom, dad, and grandma communicated with Ronnie. For sure we stomped on the floor a lot to draw Ronnie's attention. We did the same with Bobby, who was hard of hearing. Perhaps through fingerspelling my sisters (and our parents?) communicated more. This is probably why I am embarrassed to say I recall very little about Ronnie except his earning the rank of Eagle Scout, his massive, meticulously organized international stamp collection, and his bringing a Volkswagen Beetle into our family.

As strange as it may be, it has taken reaching retirement age to realize how insensitive our family was to Ronnie's communication needs. With more time came more awareness of the importance of family and friends. This has meant reaching out more to my siblings, many of whom, like Ronnie and Kay, are now well into their eighties. This increased contact with Ronnie and Kay, in particular, has opened my eyes to a brother largely unknown to me and probably to all our other family members.

In 2015, our family attended Ronnie's San Francisco Main Library one-man show displaying many newsletter covers he designed and printed as a teenager. His first book was the first book by a member of our family, and we attended his talks. We were also amazed when Ronnie served as the chairperson of the 2005 National Conference of Deaf Seniors of America in San Francisco, which was a huge success. After many years of contributing to the Deaf community, Ronnie was inducted into the California School for the Deaf Heritage Hall of Fame. And finally, in 2017, he unveiled a statue in honor of Dr. Delight Rice in the Philippine Islands at the Philippine School for the Deaf, an achievement he initiated and then helped manage and fund.

Like many in the family, I have been slow to connect all of these in a body of life work that has been amazing. This new awareness has led to more engagement with Ronnie and to my taking ASL classes. There is much more ground to cover.

That said, rather than just an introduction to his book, this should serve as an apology to Ronnie — an open apology for not having paid more attention to nor having communicated with my eldest brother, who has realized more in his lifetime by his sheer will than many of us ever will. In the process, he has immeasurably added to our three generations of American legacy.

Finally, it reminds me how in an Asian family the first-born male child is the most esteemed position that brings special responsibilities and privileges that the other siblings don't always enjoy. It also brings high hopes. Our parents never pushed us to achieve; instead, they simply taught us to respect others, elders especially, and to work and study hard without complaints. Some may also say we are programmed with these traits. If so, Ronnie was doubly endowed.

It is my hope that this book will help enlighten us all to Ronald Masato Hirano's remarkable life, and in so doing, gain him our respect and gratitude for his life's work. I thank my brother for unwaveringly fulfilling the promise of an esteemed first-born son.

Daniel Shinobu Hirano

ACKNOWLEDGMENTS

I would like to extend a heartfelt appreciation to the following people who provided invaluable assistance in making this book possible.

- **Alice Hagemeyer**, activist, library services for Deaf people
- **Newby Ely**, researcher, writer, and presenter on Deaf incarceration camp internees
- **Joyce Ingraham**, genealogist
- **Lu Ann Sleeper**, videotape interviewer, University of California
- **Daniel Hirano**, videotape interviewer of our mother at her Berkeley residence
- **Michael Olson**, archivist, Gallaudet University archives
- **Orkideh Sassouni**, librarian, Deaf Services of San Francisco Public Library
- **Jerry Kaspner**, librarian, Deaf Services of San Francisco Public Library
- **Melvin Pedersen**, historical museum curator, California School for the Deaf
- **Anita Ortiz Ner**, alumna, Philippine School for the Deaf
- **Renato Cruz**, alumnus, Philippine School for the Deaf
- **Chuck Hom**, alumnus, California School for the Deaf and Gallaudet University
- **Christian "CriCri" Gremaud**, communication leader, Swiss Federation of the Deaf in Zurich, Switzerland
- **Victor Palenny**, guide, author, and leader, Moscow, Russia
- **Nikolay Suslov**, guide and art instructor, Saint Petersburg, Russia

- **Febe Servilla**, staff interpreter, DLS-CSB, SDEAS, Manila, Philippines
- **Peggy Prosser** and **Meri Hirose**, guides, D-Travel Agency, Tokyo, Japan
- **Tomoko Yoshioka**, producer of special NHK EDU programs, NHK television station, Tokyo, Japan
- **Angela Fer** and **Lourdes Garcia**, guides and hosts, D-Travel Agency, Havana, Cuba
- **Trudy Suggs**, owner, T.S. Writing Services and Savory Words Publishing

ACRONYMS

ASL: American Sign Language
BAADA: Bay Area Asian Deaf Association
BACDSC: Bay Area Coalition of Deaf Senior Citizens
CAD: California Association of the Deaf
CAPCD: CAP College for the Deaf
CSD: California School for the Deaf
CSDAA: California School for the Deaf Alumni Association
CSDR: California School for the Deaf Riverside
DLS-CSB: De La Salle-College of Saint Benilde (simply CSB)
DLS-CSB, SDEAS: De La Salle-College of Saint Benilde, School of Deaf Education and Applied Studies
DSA: Deaf Seniors of America
EBCD: East Bay Club of the Deaf
ICDA: International Catholic Deaf Association
JSL: Japanese Sign Language (*Nihon Shuwa*)
NAD: National Association of the Deaf
NFSD: National Fraternal Society of the Deaf
NTID: National Technical Institute for the Deaf
PSD: Philippine School for the Deaf
PSDAAA: Philippine School for the Deaf Alumni Affairs Association
SFCD: San Francisco Club of the Deaf (now San Francisco Deaf Club)
SWCID: SouthWest Colligate Institute for the Deaf (now SouthWest College for the Deaf)
WFD: World Federation of the Deaf

JAPANESE TERMINOLOGY

GENERATIONS

- **Nikkei**: Americans of Japanese ancestry or Japanese-Americans in general
- **Kibei**: Person born in the U.S. of Japanese immigrant parents and educated chiefly in Japan (*such as author's mother*)
- **Issei**: First generation of immigrants from Japan (a*uthor's grandparents and father*)
- **Nisei**: Second generation of Japanese-Americans (*author's mother*)
- **Sansei**: Third generation of Japanese-Americans (*author and his siblings*)
- **Yonsei**: Fourth generation of Japanese-Americans (*children of author's siblings*)
- **Gosei**: Fifth generation of Japanese-Americans (*grandchildren of author's siblings*)

GENERAL

- **Arigato**: Thank you
- **Banzai**: Patriotic cheer or salutation
- **Diet**: Parliament
- **Enryo**: Hold back one, not two
- **Karate**: Martial art of unarmed combat of smashes, chops and kicks
- **Katana**: Long, curved single-edge samurai sword
- **Kimono**: Traditional garment and national dress
- **Koto**: Traditional musical instrument

- **Nakasendō**: One thousand-year-old highway, 332 miles, between Edo (now Tokyo) and Kyoto
- **Nihonmachi**: Japantown
- **NHK**: National television network
- **Ryōkan**: Inn offering traditional cuisine, furnishings and large communal baths
- **Samurai**: Professional swordsman, representing feudal military aristocracy
- **Sayonara**: Farewell
- **Shikata ga nai**: Code of silence; it cannot be helped or nothing can be done about it.

CHAPTER 1

Previous page:

A young Mary Morioka, Ron's mother.

CHAPTER 1
EARLY FAMILYHOOD (1871-1932)

THE HIRANO FAMILY

My paternal grandmother Ina Watanabe (1874-1981) was born to Gensaburo and Yasu Watanabe in Sendai, Miyagi Prefecture in central Japan. Her family once was wealthy, but lost money, which forced Ina to ultimately work as a maid in a military general's residence. The general introduced her to a military man, Hanakichi Hirano (1871-1920), whom she married in 1902. They lived in Nagano Prefecture in the region of Japan Alps, where their first child James Shigeo (1903-1984) was born. In 1905, Hanakichi left for California in search of work. Emigrating from the port of Yokohama in 1909,

Front: Oshu, Yone, and Jiro (Jack). Center: Grandma Ina and James. Back: Grandpa Hanakichi. West Oakland, CA, circa 1915.

James and his mother Ina joined Hanakichi in San Francisco on December 17, 1909 via the passenger ship *Tenyo Maru*. They eventually established a cleaner/laundry and bathhouse business on Seventh Street and Market Street near a railroad station in West Oakland. They went on to bear Yone (nee Yuasa) (1910-2009), Jiro "Jack" (1912-1998), and Oshu (nee

3

Ikoma) (1914-1997). James wanted to attend college badly, but he couldn't afford tuition. After Hanakichi passed at the relatively young age of forty-nine in 1920, James' forty-five-year-old mother Ina took over the family business. The seventeen-year-old James then became the family patriarch according to Japanese custom.

Front: Jiro (Jack), Oshu and Yone; Back: Hanakichi, James, and Ina. West Oakland, CA, circa 1919.

The family attended the Tenth Street Methodist Church, which provided services in Japanese and English. It was located on the corner of Tenth Street and Castro Street in West Oakland. James supervised church events such as parties, weddings and funerals. The church clan was self-segregated and members of various families intermarried.

THE MORIOKA FAMILY

In Hiroshima Prefecture in the southern region of Japan, George Shiro Morioka (1882-1945) was born as the fourth child of Chuzaemon Morioka Jr. (1842-1914) and Tona Yoshioka (1848-1907). After spending six years working on a pineapple plantation in Hawaii, Shiro came to San Francisco right after Great Earthquake of 1906 and worked as a laborer. In typical Japanese custom, he asked his parents to seek a prospective bride. They mailed him a photo of Fuji Hata (1887-1958), who had left her husband and monk Sakichi Takeda and her daughter Takae, now Suzuki, after clashing with her sister-in-law. Her parents were Tomokichi Hata and Mitsu Murakami. She met and married Shiro in San Francisco in 1905. They bore Mary Shizue (nee Hirano) (1909-2000) and Masae (nee

4

The Hirano Family, L-R: Oshu, Ina, Yone, James and Jiro (Jack).
West Oakland, CA, circa 1927.

Sato) (1910-2001) at a Victorian residence on Cook Street near Geary Street. The Great Depression had a heavy impact on them. In 1911, Fuji took two-year-old Mary and one-year-old Masae to Innoshima near Hiroshima in Japan to be reared by Fuji's mother and uncle respectively. Shiro was employed as a houseboy and Fuji did domestic work. Yoshiko "Yoshi" (nee Nakano) (1912-2006), Fred Toshio (1914-2007), and May Fumiko (nee Okamoto) (1917-2015), were successively born.

In 1918, Shiro and Fuji started a dry-cleaning business, Sun Cleaning & Drying Company, on 1640 Gough Street in Western Addition. The business, renamed Sun Cleaner, later moved to Sacramento Street between Van Ness Avenue and Polk Street in Polk Gulch. It eventually expanded to a second location on Lombard Street in Cow Hollow.

Mary Morioka and   *Shiro and Fuji Morioka.*
Grandma Mitsu Hata.

In 1923, the U.S. Congress passed the Asian Exclusion Act banning further immigration from Asian countries, so the alarmed parents decided to recall Mary and Masae from Japan after twelve years. In June 1923, fourteen-year-old Mary and thirteen-year-old Masae were taken to the Seto Inland Sea port of Kobe (Hyōgo Port) for sailing home. But Mary was detained because of tapeworms in her stomach. So Masae sailed alone and arrived at San Francisco on June 23, 1923 on *Tenyo Maru.* In late August 1923, Mary finally embarked on a passenger ship at the port of Kobe. The ship later stopped at the port of Yokohama near Tokyo for refueling and boarding additional cargo and passengers. During the stopover, Mary shopped around and went to a movie with a friend at the port city. On September 1, 1923, Tokyo was struck by Great Kantō Earthquake at a magnitude of 7.9, triggering a massive firestorm and causing 105,000 deaths. As the ship pulled away from the burning dock and port, Mary witnessed that deadly apocalypse. Amid the chaos, the Moriokas worried about Mary. She reached San Francisco safely on October 1, 1923. Mary and

Masae were then sent to school to learn English. They never got along well with their American-cultured siblings, and that tension endured throughout their lives.

To accommodate their five children, Shiro and Fuji bought and renovated a rundown two-story, twelve-room Victorian residence at 1923 Bush Street in Nihonmachi. They brought in roomers to help pay the mortgage. After a few years, they gradually acquired commercial and residential properties in San Francisco.

HISTORICAL FACT:
EMIGRATION FROM JAPAN

In 1868, Emperor Meiji (1852-1912) promoted the westernization of Japan, ending medieval feudalism and generating immense poverty among the rural population. In 1885, the imperial government began to sponsor emigration programs in order to alleviate overpopulation, agricultural deflation, and impoverishment. Emigrants from Japan, known as *Issei*, traveled to Brazil, Canada, Peru and the United States.

Upon entry at customs, Asian immigrants were examined, searched and released, and sometimes detained and quarantined at Angel Island—often called Ellis Island of the West—in the foggy, windy strait of Golden Gate near San Francisco.

In 1905, the Imperial Japan's naval victory over Imperial Russia in the Russo-Japanese War spread xenophobia to the Pacific Coast. As a result, the California Alien Land Law of 1913 prohibited Issei from owning property. Racial discrimination against Nikkei prevented integration and assimilation until after World War II.

CHAPTER 2

Previous pages:
The Hirano family residence from 1932 until 1942
at 2809 California Street in Berkeley, California.

CHAPTER 2
CHILDHOOD
(1932-1941)

James Hirano was introduced to Mary Morioka and her sisters by his longtime friend George Furuta. Her family did not like James so Mary was relegated to phone conversations with James. Eventually, Mary converted from Buddhism to Methodism, and James and Mary were married at the Tenth Street Methodist Church on January 31, 1932. They spent their first night as a married couple at Hotel Claremont in Berkeley and then honeymooned at Yosemite National Park and at a Little Tokyo hotel in Los Angeles. Upon return from their honeymoon, they rented a Mediterranean-style three-bedroom, one-bathroom single family house at 2809 California Street in West Berkeley. While living there, they bore three children: me, Robert "Bobby" Shigenobu (1934-present), and Janet Inako (1938-present). Grandmother Ina resided with them.

James and Mary Hirano were married on January 31, 1932.

I was born profoundly deaf on November 28, 1932. Mary named me after her favorite movie actor Ronald Colman. A physician, upon learning that I was deaf, advised my parents to consult Delight Rice, the hearing daughter of Deaf parents. Shortly after, my younger brother Bobby was diagnosed as hard of hearing. Delight recommended that my parents enroll me at California School for the Deaf in Berkeley and Bobby at Gough School for the Oral Deaf in San Francisco once we reached school age. That was the beginning of my cherished lifelong relationship with Delight.

Author Ronald Hirano in 1932.

When young, I often curiously observed my mother's koto ritual. Kneeling on the living room floor, she practiced playing the koto. Made of kiri wood and seventy-one inches long, the koto had twelve strings connected over thirteen movable bridges along the width of the instrument. She occasionally played it at church. I was also captivated by my father's daily task of taking down his heirloom katana from its living room wall mount, removing the sheath, and oiling, powdering, and polishing it. During the evacuation order in the spring of 1942, FBI agents confiscated it, and it was never returned. I imagine if we still had it in the family, it would be priceless.

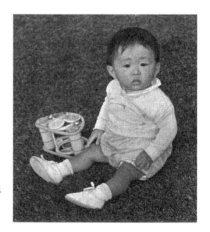

Ron in 1933.

From time to time starting when I was seven years old, Delight came to pick me up and drive me to East Bay Club of the Deaf on Franklin Street in downtown Oakland. I recall seeing a row of legal slot machines there at one point. At the club, I became acquainted with friendly Deaf people

*Ron with his parents
and Granny Ina in 1933.*

*Bobby and Ron
in 1937.*

*Ron's family at Neptune Beach in
Alameda, California in 1937.*

*Ron at Neptune Beach,
this time in 1939.*

Ron, Janet, and Bobby in 1940.

Ron in 1940.

The Hirano family in 1941.
L-R (Back): Hachiro and Yone Yuasa, Janet, and James
and Mary Hirano. L-R (Front): Ron and Bobby.

and was immersed in Deaf culture and American Sign Language (ASL).

To get us out of the house, my parents often took us to the nearby Tilden Regional Park for a picnic. We also went swimming at the now-defunct Neptune Beach amusement park, which operated from 1917 to 1939 at the end of Webster Street in Alameda. My family occasionally rode the Key System H train along Sacramento Street one block from our California Street residence to the bay ferry terminal in West Oakland.

Ron, Bobby, and Janet in 1941.

After ferrying across the bay, we transferred to the Ferry Terminal in San Francisco and then rode on Muni streetcars along the four-track Market Street downtown for shopping. Crossing the newly-completed San Francisco-Oakland Bay Bridge, my parents often took us to attend the Golden Gate International Exposition on Treasure Island in 1939-1940, a contemporary of the New York World Fair. It was built on a 575-acre artificial island filled by mud, sand, and rocks from caissons for bridge foundations. On Sunday afternoons, James loved to drive us around leisurely browsing at homes on Berkeley Hills overlooking San Francisco and its surrounding bay. He dreamed about the possible purchase of one of those in the near future.

One of my father's many jobs was being a salesman for an import retail store in San Francisco. I was once told that he was one of the top salesmen there, even going on several buying trips to Japan. When the Depression ended that job, he held various jobs, including chicken sexing, a method of distinguishing the sex of chickens, and gardening. He eventually opened a produce market on Fourteenth Street between Franklin Street and Webster Street in downtown Oakland, while his brother Jack managed another one in the predominantly white Elmhurst district of East Oakland near the now-defunct General Motors assembly facility.

In 1940, my father and we children were injured in a freak accident, as described in an article excerpted from the September 9 issue of the *Oakland Tribune*.

BERKELEY, Sept. 9—Two freak accidents here yesterday sent five persons to Berkeley hospital for treatment.

Most seriously injured were James Hirano, 36, of 2809 California Street and his three children, Ronald, 6, Janet, 2, and Robert, 5.

They were standing on the sidewalk in front of their home when an automobile driven by Richard V. Ranft, 19, 1603 McGee Street, rounded the corner of California and Oregon Streets.

A front tire blew out, sending the auto hurtling over the curb, narrowly missing Hirano and his children. The car hit the front steps of their house, and then bounced back and struck them.

Hirano suffered bruises. Robert had cuts and bruises, shock and second-degree friction burns; Janet, abrasions of the scalp, and Ronald, cuts about the face.

Police investigated a possibility of reckless driving.

My father later drove me down to Los Angeles to attend the wedding of his brother Jack and Emy Odanaka. We left my mother and Janet at home because Bobby was hospitalized after stomach surgery. My father showed me a hotel in Little Tokyo where he and my mother had honeymooned. It was not until the early 2000s, at my Aunt Emy's memorial service in Ignacio, that I first saw a family photograph from the wedding that showed my father and me.

Shortly before the Pearl Harbor attack on December 7, 1941, my father sold the produce market. By coincidence of his sale, rumors circulated among Japanese community in Bay Area that he might be a spy. Afterward, Uncle Jack was forced to sell his business at a fire sale. According to Bobby, our father was detained and questioned by FBI for spying, but this account has yet to be authenticated.

HISTORICAL FACTS:
NIHONMACHI

Nihonmachi was founded by Issei during the late nineteenth century and the early twentieth century. Statewide, forty-three of them were built, but they were devastated by wartime incarceration in the spring of 1942. After the war, only three survived: San Francisco, San Jose, and Los Angeles. Prior to the 1906 earthquake, San Francisco had two Nihonmachi, one near Chinatown and another in South of Market. Afterward, it was relocated to Western Addition.

CALIFORNIA FARMS

In the late nineteenth century, Issei began farming the fertile land in California. This continued even after they returned home from relocation camps after the war. Their farms flourished, serving an important part in California's agribusiness.

CALIFORNIA SCHOOL FOR THE DEAF

Upon recommendation by Delight, my parents enrolled me at CSD in Berkeley at the age of five. On the first day, I shyly approached, gradually played, curiously gestured, and then became warmly acquainted with peers. After a short time, I keenly grasped and then mastered ASL. The language enabled me to converse effectively with staff and teachers. Logically, I immersed in education as well as culture. I found and cherished fellowship in the school. As a day pupil, I commuted less than two miles between my home and the residential school,

California School for the Deaf, Berkeley, 1930.

which meant I didn't stay in the dormitories like so many other students at the time. But this didn't exclude me from the many fun pranks we pulled on each other. A third-grade classmate once asked me to sign "pulling out a drawer." I answered correctly, but was told that I was being indecent. It was only later that I realized he had manipulated me into using an obscene gesture that indicated sexual intercourse. How embarrassed and naive I felt!

One day, Delight picked me up and drove twenty miles northward to Vallejo to visit the politically prominent parents of a Deaf child, Daniel Lynch. She convinced his mother to enroll him at CSD much to Daniel's pleasure, even though the mother supported oralism instead of ASL.

*Students at the California School for the Deaf in 1940;
Ron is in the center foreground.*

*Students at the California School for the Deaf in 1940;
Ron is in front at far left.*

HISTORICAL FACT:
CALIFORNIA SCHOOL FOR THE DEAF

California School for the Deaf opened on May 1, 1860 with its first class of three pupils at a rented house at 15 Tehama Street in downtown San Francisco, a location now covered by skyscrapers. Within six months, its enrollment increased to sixteen, so a new schoolhouse was a necessity. In 1861, it finally moved to a newly built site on the corner of Mission Street and Sparks (now Sixteenth) Street in Mission District, where the BART Station is today situated. Three years later, the school outgrew that facility with thirty-three pupils, but it wasn't until 1869 that the school relocated to a 130-acre campus on Warring Street and Parker Street in Berkeley across the bay. The state also began supporting the school financially. Classes were taught from kindergarten through the twelfth grade using a combined method of ASL and lipreading and speech. In 1980, the school moved to its current 91-acre site on Gallaudet Drive and Stevenson Street in Fremont, thirty miles south of Berkeley. The school, now accredited, today practices a bilingual approach of ASL and English, and offers education from early-start toddler classes to high school.

ASIAN ALUMNI LEGENDS OF
THE CALIFORNIA SCHOOL FOR THE DEAF

Lillian Hahn Skinner (1919-2000)
Class of 1934

- 1939 Gallaudet College graduate
- First board chairperson of California Home for Aged Deaf (circa 1980)
- President of California Association of the Deaf (1975-1977)
- President of Hollywood Club of the Deaf (circa 1960)
- President of Los Angeles Club of the Deaf (circa 1950)
- First chairlady of the nineteenth annual National Basketball Tournament of American Athletic Association of the Deaf (1963)
- President, Farwest Athletic Association of the Deaf (1956 and 1961)

Shanny Mow (1938-2015)
Class of 1956

- 1961 Gallaudet University graduate
- Director of artistic development for Cleveland Signstage Theatre (1990-1996)
- Director of several original and established plays for over twenty years
- Professional playwright of over twenty-four plays (1976-2006)
- Faculty member for National Theater of the Deaf (NTD) Professional School
- Director of the Deaf Playwrights Conference at NTD
- Artistic Director of Fairmount Theatre of the Deaf in Cleveland, Ohio
- Actor at NTD (1978-1980 and 1985-1987)
- Teacher at Montana, New Mexico, and Hawaii Schools for the Deaf

CHAPTER 3

Previous pages:
A New Year's Eve celebration at East Bay Club of the Deaf in Oakland, California on December 31, 1942. Ron and Delight Rice are in the front at left.

24

CHAPTER 3
THE WAR YEARS
(1941-1945)

On the quiet evening of December 7, 1941, I observed my father listening to the radio in the kitchen. He suddenly screamed and then cried. I asked him what happened, but he did not answer. I was clueless until the next morning when I read the newspaper about the Pearl Harbor attack. I was stunned.

Delight Rice and Ron in 1943.

Due to an imminent evacuation in the early spring of 1942, my father James asked Delight to take over guardianship of me because he perceived relocation camps as lacking educational opportunities for me as a Deaf child. She obliged, and offered to take Bobby along with me, but James refused because of the Japanese custom of *enryo* (restraint). Delight then obtained a special permit from the FBI for me in case law enforcement ever requested proof.

In March 1942, I moved to Delight's two-story, four-bedroom, two-bathroom residence on 2149 Blake Street in Berkeley. This was a significant change to my life. After all, until now, I had been raised in a household reflecting Nikkei family culture. In contrast, the Rice family household engaged in Caucasian customs. Second, unlike nutritious American and Japanese dishes prepared by my mother, Delight cooked what I thought were quite bland meals, such as cornmeal, porridge, casseroles, and stews. Finally, all of the hearing Rice family members were fluent signers, while nobody in my family aside from my brother signed. This was a positive change in my life, because I now had 24-hour access to communication at home.

Ron at the age of 11 in 1944.

In April 1942, buses lined up along Durant Street in Berkeley, ready to pick up Nikkei evacuees to transport them to assembly centers. Delight drove me to bid *sayonara* to my family there. (Many years later, my siblings told me that I unconsciously snubbed my mother, for reasons I am not clear about.) The internees were transported across the bay to Tanforan Assembly Center in San Bruno, ten miles south of San Francisco. The center was temporarily converted from a racetrack to accommodate eight thousand evacuees from all over Northern California.

A month later, Delight took me to visit my family at Tanforan. We were shocked to find them housed in horse stables. My parents introduced us to Tadashi "Tad" Yamamoto, a 1938 CSD graduate, who they had graciously given extra clothing and accessories. Tad told me his terrifying story of residing alone in an apartment in Oakland, unaware of the posted evacuation order in February 1942. One night, FBI agents barged into the apartment, quickly hauled him out without packing, and drove him directly to Tanforan—all the while he had no idea what was happening. After the war, I

HISTORICAL FACT:
INCARCERATION OF NIKKEI

On December 7, 1941, the Imperial Japanese attack upon Pearl Harbor in Hawaii quickly triggered a wave of panic along the west coast. On February 19, 1942, President Franklin D. Roosevelt issued the now-infamous Executive Order 9066 authorizing the incarceration of 120,000 Nikkei residents of California, Oregon, Washington, and Alaska. Sixty-five percent of the Nikkei residents were legal U.S. citizens. Nikkei Canadian families were also sent to internment camps in British Columbia.

From Peru in coastal South America, Nisei families were evacuated to internment camps in the United States. There was no repercussion for Americans of German and Italian ancestry. To this day, no single Nikkei was ever prosecuted for nor convicted of any espionage against the United States.

Ironically, Nikkei in Hawaii were not interned because they comprised more than a third of the population and were the second largest ethnic group. If they had been interned, the Hawaiian economy would have collapsed.

To prove loyalty to the United States, Nisei and Sansei volunteered to join the segregated yet famed 2nd Battalion, 442nd Regimental Combat Team, the most decorated in U.S. Army history. Recruited from internment camps, Nisei were stationed at Military Intelligence Service in Minnesota as translators and also were posted in the Pacific theater as interpreters. In 2010, the Congressional Gold Medal was awarded to six thousand Nisei of such units.

Ron's family was interned at Topaz Relocation Camp in Utah.

occasionally encountered Tad at East Bay Club of the Deaf in Oakland, and he repeatedly told me of his heartfelt gratitude for my parents' generosity. He passed away in the 1970s.

In September 1942, my family, along with eight thousand other internees, were again transported—this time, by train—from Tanforan to Topaz Relocation Camp near the small town of Delta in the desolate region of Western-Central Utah. This hastily-built camp consisted of forty-two blocks, each of which had twelve rows of barracks with a mess hall, a latrine and a laundry, a recreation hall and an office for a block manager at its center. Each barrack was further divided into six rooms heated by coal stoves. My father James was elected as a block manager, and my parents worked in the mess kitchen.

Unlike prison—despite being surrounded by high barbed-wired fences and watchtowers—Topaz housed two elementary schools, a high school, and an administration center. The newspaper *Topaz Times* chronicled camp life, and described how the camp was self-sufficient by farming and raising livestock. Internees were permitted to depart from the camp for the Midwest and East. During the camp, Topaz was Utah's fifth largest city.

My second brother, Daniel Shinobu (1942-present), was born at Delta Hospital, now Delta Community Medical Center

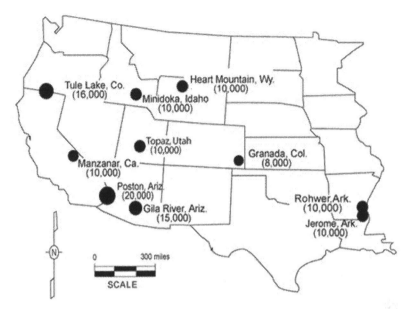

A map showing the Japanese-American internment camps in the west.

*Ron visited his mother (left) and grandma (right)
at Topaz Relocation Camp in the winter of 1943.*

The Hirano family in 1943.

Delight Rice with the Hirano family at Topaz in 1944. Ron is in the back at left.

A Salt Lake Tribune *reporter drew the Hirano family at Topaz. (L-R): Ina, Bobby, Daniel, James, Mary and Janet.*

near the internment camp, because a camp hospital had not been built yet. My second sister, Carol Aiko (1944-present), was born at the Topaz hospital. In December 1943, Mr. Miller, who was active at the Tenth Street Methodist Church before the war, took me by train to visit my family at Topaz. In the summer of 1944, when I was eleven years old, Delight accompanied me to see the family at Topaz. She went to Delta to shop, tore off stamps from her war ration book to purchase restricted foods, and generously gave them to my family. My father also helped Kazuko "Kay" Momii, a Deaf internee, enroll at Utah School for the Deaf in Ogden. In August 1945, internees were released from the camp — but my grandfather, Shiro Morioka, had recently passed away at the age of sixty-three at the camp hospital. Meanwhile, the Pacific War came to an end.

The Morioka Family in 1944. Grandma Fuji and Yoshi stand behind Grandpa Shiro.

During wartime, as a history buff, I watched weekly newsreels at Telenews Theater in downtown Oakland. I read daily newspapers, tracking the ever-changing front lines in both European and Pacific campaigns and marked them on large maps posted on my bedroom wall.

Delight captivated me with issues in the international Deaf community. For instance, she told me of the infamous 1880 Second International Congress on Education of the Deaf in Milan, Italy. At this conference, the 164 delegates—only one was Deaf—overwhelmingly passed a resolution banning sign language and implementing oral education worldwide. The self-declared inventor of the telephone, Alexander Graham Bell (1847-1922), was a fluent signer with a non-signing deaf wife and a non-signing deaf mother. He was notoriously instrumental in the outcome of the conference. After 130 years of wreaking devastation upon deaf education, in 2010, the twenty-first International Congress on Education of Deaf in Vancouver, British Columbia, Canada, formally rescinded the ban with an apology.

Delight also taught me about George Veditz (1861-1937), the seventh president of National Association of the Deaf (1904-1910). Veditz was deeply troubled about the threat of the advancement of oral method in schools. Furthermore, he persistently campaigned for the preservation of ASL and created a film project recording signing speeches by renowned Deaf leaders. His prominent 1913 speech was as follows:

As long as we have Deaf people on earth, we will have signs. And as long as we have our films, we can preserve signs in their old purity. It is my hope that we will all love and guard our beautiful sign language as the noblest gift God has given to Deaf people.

The vintage films are archived in the Library of Congress in Washington, DC, and continue to serve a crucial role in preservation of sign language.

Delight further shared that, in the 1920s, an educator from Clarke School for the Deaf, now Clarke School for Hearing and Speech, in Northampton, Massachusetts petitioned Diet (the Japanese Parliament), to outlaw sign language and to advocate the oral method at Deaf schools in Japan. In 2011, Japanese Sign Language was officially recognized.

One day, Delight had to call Walter Lester (1881-1962), the Deaf owner of a plumbing business, to repair a clogged sewer pipe in her front yard. I helped him dig up a trench and was gifted with learning some plumbing tricks. Walter and his wife, Isabel MacDonald (1881-1966), both 1901 CSD graduates, were presidents of California Association of the Deaf (1948-1950 and 1927-1931, respectively). They were people I admired.

When I was eight, Uncle Hachiro gave me a small album and a packet of stamps. I naively glued them into the album. Eventually, Delight taught me how to mount them properly. Long-time philatelist Walter Lester also sold stamps to me.

HISTORICAL FACT:
EXPULSION OF NIKKEI STUDENTS

In April 1942, Teruko Kubotsu, Kazuko Momii, Hannah Takagi, and Ikeda siblings Annabelle, Rosie and Ernest were expulsed from CSD and sent to interment camps. In the fall of 1945, they returned to the school, although Annabelle and Rosie eventually left after struggling with academics. Ernest, Teruko, and Kazuko later obtained diplomas from CSD. Ernest and Teruko went on to graduate from Gallaudet College. Hannah attended the Illinois School for the Deaf in Jacksonville.

Worldwide, a high volume of new issues overwhelmed me so I switched to specialize in stamps of sports and first-day covers, a hobby I continue today.

SECONDARY EDUCATION
California School for the Deaf

During wartime, I commuted less than a mile between Delight's residence and CSD. I was ridiculed by my schoolmates with racial slurs such as "Jap!" But I once outsmarted and silenced a foul-mouthed student with an Italian surname simply because he didn't know how to respond to my retorts. I also became friends with a peer of German ancestry, largely because of the Axis alliance of Nazi Germany, Fascist Italy and Imperial Japan.

I was an ambitious entrepreneur. When I was eleven, I purchased a box of candy bars at a discount at Penny Saver Market at the corner of Shattuck Avenue and Haste Street in downtown Berkeley. I then resold them for a decent profit to students viewing the Saturday night movie at the old CSD administration auditorium.

The fourth-grade class at the California School for the Deaf in 1943-1944. Ron is in front at far right.

The fifth-grade class at the California School for the Deaf in 1944-1945. Ron is in back at far right.

In third through sixth grades, I was very short compared to my peers. Delight took me to a specialist for a growth hormone therapy, and I gradually grew to a normal height of 5'7".

In 1944, sports enthusiasts, including me, excitedly met and chatted with a short, portly and elderly gentleman William "Dummy" Hoy (1862-1961) visiting CSD. He had graduated from Ohio School for the Deaf as class valedictorian in 1879. He opened a shoe repair shop in his small hometown of Houcktown and played baseball on weekends. In 1886, he began playing for a professional baseball team in Oshkosh, Wisconsin. From 1888 to 1902, he became the first Deaf outfielder for several professional baseball teams, notably the Cincinnati Reds. Today, Hoy is credited with having devised a system of hand signals still used by umpires today. Hoy was also as an executive with Goodyear Tire & Rubber Company in Akron, Ohio, supervising several hundred Deaf workers during World War I. A committee has been campaigning for his induction into the National Baseball Hall of Fame and Museum in Cooperstown, New York.

At the age of twelve, I was examined by a doctor at CSD. He diagnosed rheumatic fever and he prohibited me from participating in sports. I was so upset that I complained to Delight, who had me re-examined by another physician. I was given a clean slate, much to my happiness.

OTHER SCHOOLS

Delight enrolled me in a summer art class at Longfellow Middle School in Berkeley. I was one of a few boys in a class of girls. During class break, I unintentionally followed the female teacher leading the girls into their restroom. When one of the girls saw me and screamed, I immediately ran out of there. It continues to be one of the most embarrassing experiences in my life.

On Saturdays and summer days, I attended the California College of the Arts in Oakland. I took an art course in charcoal and pastel sketching and watercolor painting.

Previous pages:
*The Bear Hunt statue was sculpted by Douglas Tilden, a sculptor
who was Deaf. It stands at the front of California School for the Deaf in
Fremont.*

CHAPTER 4
POST-WAR YEARS (1945-1952)

In July 1945, my father James returned to the Bay Area to inspect family assets stored at Tenth Street Methodist Church in Oakland and other properties in San Francisco. The following month, my family and other internees finally departed Topaz and returned to Northern California. My family lived at 1923 Bush Street in Nihonmachi in San Francisco and had a few Nikkei roomers.

Sharing a front room at the Bush Street residence, my father ran three successive businesses: gardening, an income tax service, and finally importing Oriental interior decorations under the business name of United Enterprises. When the company outgrew its office in 1970, he relocated the company to a newly purchased warehouse on Alabama Street in the Mission District. He often went to Japan on buying trips, purchasing vintage items off the beaten path, and reselling

HISTORICAL FACT:
RETURNING FROM THE CAMPS

Some Nikkei were able to arrange for their property and possessions to be protected by friends and neighbors. For many others returning from the camps, they found their properties either dispossessed or looted. They resumed restoring real estate from scratch like their ancestors had fifty years earlier.

them to interior decorators with wealthy clients such as Gordon Getty, Bob Hope, and Barbara Hutton.

On July 9, 1947, Delight drove me 250 miles south to Paso Robles to house-sit for her friends traveling overseas for three weeks. The small town in Salinas Valley was well known for its wineries and olive and almond orchards. We visited nearby Salinas, Monterey, and Carmel. On July 14, we went to Los Angeles to attend a convention of the now-defunct National Fraternal Society of the Deaf (NFSD). I met and chatted

The Hirano family in 1949.
(L-R): Ron, Bobby, Janet, Daniel,
Carol, and Gordon.

with the friendly NFSD Canadian Vice President, David Peikoff, who now has the Gallaudet University Alumni House named after him and his wife. Taking me to this convention was just one way Delight continually exposed me to the important organizations and events of the Deaf community, showing me Deaf leaders in action.

When my mother became pregnant again, my father decided to name the infant Delight Rice if it was a girl. On August 30, 1947, a boy was born so he was named Gordon Rice. I personally wanted his name to be Charles Rice because it was the first name of several Rice males. For example, Delight's father was Charles Merrick Rice, her brother, Charles Freeman Rice, her nephew, Charles "Buddy" Sutton Rice, and her grand-nephew, Charles "Beau" Beauregard Rice.

Until 1951, I alternated between Delight's house in Berkeley on weekdays and my family's residence in San Francisco on weekends. Delight retired from the Berkeley Public Schools in 1949 after more than twenty years as an

Ron's family went to dinner to celebrate his graduation from CSD in 1952. (L-R): Bobby, Mary, James, and Ron.

audiologist and moved to Southern California to become an audiological consultant at the Hearing Center of Metropolitan Los Angeles.

I occasionally shopped at the now-closed Palmer's Drug Store in Shattuck Square in downtown Berkeley. Once, I was leisurely browsing a long rack of periodicals and reading a magazine. Suddenly, an enraged elderly man shouted closely at my ear and then pointed down at a dime he dropped that was under my shoe. I noticed a crowd of people staring at me, and I became so embarrassed that I signaled to him that I was Deaf. Apparently, he had tried to talk to me from behind without tapping on my shoulder.

During family gatherings, I amicably debated politics, such as capitalism and socialism with Uncle Hachiro, who was a hard-core socialist, by scribbling and passing notes back and forth. As a fast, skillful player, he usually defeated me in various table games such as Chinese and American checkers, and chess.

During the 1950-53 Korean War, males were required to register for enlistment once they became eighteen years old.

I ignored that requirement because I was Deaf. Much to my surprise, I received a draft notice when I was nineteen. The examiner at the nearby draft office was angry at me and did not initially believe that I was Deaf. He repeatedly tried to force me to speak and lipread and asked me numerous questions through written communication. He finally accepted that I was indeed Deaf and issued me a draft card stamped Class 4F, deeming me ineligible for military service.

CALIFORNIA SCHOOL FOR THE DEAF

Just six years after the incorporation of Boy Scouts of America (BSA), a troop was formed at CSD in 1916. In early 1945, I joined Troop 11 as a tenderfoot, and successively advanced through the ranks of assistant patrol leader, patrol leader, senior patrol leader and finally junior assistant scoutmaster. At jamborees, we won numerous ribbons that were hung at the top of the troop flag. After collecting twenty-nine merit badges, on December 12, 1951 during an annual banquet at Berkeley Elks Club, I received the seventh Eagle Scout award in CSD history.

Ron achieved Eagle Scout rank in December 1951.

In late 1945, I was hospitalized with pneumonia at Franklin Hospital in San Francisco. A series of penicillin shots made me so sick that I lost fifteen pounds. After a month-long absence from school, I finally resumed attending classes and quickly caught up.

Every afternoon, our class took an hourly course of speech and lipreading. The classmates received good grades—but I always had low grades. I continue to have no use for speech.

I attended printing classes taught by Deaf instructors Alpha Patterson and later John Galvan. We published school periodicals such as *The California News*. Mr. Galvan once asked us what the definition of *galvanize* was. We were unfamiliar with it so he ordered us to consult a dictionary. He then boasted that his brain never rusted. I learned to use a linotype machine, set up metal printing formats, and made linocuts for publication covers. These skills served me well later in life.

At the Berkeley Theater on Shattuck Avenue between Haste Street and Dwight Way, teenage schoolmates and I customarily paid admission fees for under-twelve whenever we simply pointed at our ears to indicate that we were Deaf.

On May 2, 1946, a three-day battle occurred at the Alcatraz Federal Penitentiary in Golden Gate, sparked by a failed escape attempt. At the Moss Hall dormitory overlooking the bay and the strait, my peers and I witnessed the battle. Two guards and three convicts were killed. Two surviving convicts, Miran Thompson and Sam Shockley, were eventually executed at the nearby San Quentin State Prison.

During the 1946-47 school year, a witty, hilarious teacher, Gladys Gifford, taught our seventh-grade class, consisting of seven girls and two boys—Julian "Buddy" Singleton and me. It was one of the most memorable classes, like the time the teacher talked about female clothes like girdles or corsets. Buddy asked her what a corset was, and she quickly responded by pulling up her dress, exposing it. We were all stunned. Buddy and I reminisce about that even today. Another day, Buddy was absent, leaving me alone in the all-girls class. Ms. Gifford was once again talking about female things. She and the girls flirted with me, making me uncomfortable and embarrassed. Nowadays, this would not be acceptable behavior, but it was a different time then, and done in good-natured spirits.

Another memorable incident took place in senior class taught by renowned community leader Byron B. Burnes

*Class of 1952 sophomores at the California School
for the Deaf; Ron is in the back row at far right.*

Class of 1952 juniors; Ron is in front at far left.

Foothill Athletic Association in 1952; Ron is in front, third from left.

Ron's senior portrait in 1952.

Ron poses in his graduation gown and cap in 1952.

Ron was a defensive guard on the CSD football team.

Ron also ran the one-mile and 880-yard events in track.

(1904-1996). Buddy was playing with a firecracker as the teacher reviewed homework at his desk. Buddy lit the firecracker and attempted to throw it through an open window. The firework bounced off the window frame and exploded. Mr. Burnes, clearly stone-deaf, was completely unaware of Buddy's shenanigans regardless of the loud bang and rising smoke. He must have also lacked any sense of smell. Fortunately, nobody was hurt.

I occasionally visited the National Association of the Deaf (NAD) then-home office on the corner of Shattuck Avenue and Dwight Way, two blocks from Delight's residence. As its president, Mr. Burnes spent most of his spare time alone there when he wasn't teaching. His eighteen-year term from 1946 to 1964 remains the longest presidency in NAD history.

When I was fourteen, I began living in the school dormitory to focus on training and participating in sports. My roommates Epifanio Arce, Joseph Maxwell, Robert Scribner, and I often playfully wrestled each other in our room, pushing beds around. The burly Epifanio, an All-American football player among Deaf schools, always beat us; Robert and I alternately landed in last place.

I earned money cleaning a billiard pool in the dormitory. During football games, several schoolmates and I earned money by selling hot dogs and sodas at the nearby University of California football stadium.

I played football as a defensive guard. I also competed in track and field, where I excelled in the 880-yard and one-mile runs. I won such events at the Northern California Nisei Track Meet in San Francisco and at the Nisei Relays in Los Angeles in 1951. Several CSD schoolmates attended the Los Angeles event, and my father treated them to dinner afterwards at a Japanese restaurant.

I was the editor of the June 1952 edition of *The California News* featuring our graduating class. Possessing the nickname of Martian, I drew a cartoon of a futuristic Martian city filled with towering skyscrapers depicting our classmates.

The California Association of the Deaf Award was annually presented to a highest-ranking senior. Our class expected me to receive it. Instead, Leo Jacobs awarded it to Robert Scribner, stunning us all, including the recipient himself. I continue to believe it was because of Leo's notorious favoritism.

EMPLOYMENT: CLAREMONT PRESS PUBLISHING

During the summer in 1951, I was hired to work at Claremont Press Publishing. One night, I lost a part of my left index finger in a printing accident. My boss, Joaquim de Menezes,

Ron edited the June 1952 edition of The California News. *Note his signature on the left side of the bear statue.*

HISTORICAL FACT:
CLAREMONT PRESS PUBLISHING

Claremont Press Publishing, no longer in operation, in Oakland printed weekly local newspapers. Its commercial shop was converted from a garage and was partly hidden behind a large two-story Gothic-style residence on Telegraph Avenue. During the summers, several Deaf printers from CSD worked there.

immediately drove me to a nearby hospital and, after I was released, he took me to Delight's house in Berkeley, but she was out of town. The next morning, I went to my parents' residence in San Francisco. My parents immediately took me to Franklin Hospital, where I had my finger stump sewn up with four stitches. Rumors started to spread among the Deaf community about the accident as far as Los Angeles. The first rumor indicated I crushed an index finger; the next one, I lost a hand; then I had a hand and forearm amputated; lastly, I had an entire arm cut off.

MOROSI FINE PRINTING COMPANY

The Morosi Fine Printing owner, John Morosi, purposely employed Nikkei staff, who were known for their loyalty and hard work. This is probably why I was immediately hired during the summer break of 1952. When autumn approached, I notified the owner that I was leaving for Gallaudet College. He panicked and offered me a raise, but I refused. I did not follow the Nikkei working tradition because I was fully Americanized. However, after graduation from college in 1955, the owner quickly rehired me. I worked there for two more years while studying architecture at Heald College in San Francisco and City College of San Francisco.

CHAPTER 5

CHAPTER 5
COLLEGE YEARS (1952-1955)

Gallaudet College (which was accredited in 1955) was so small back then that all of the students knew each other. When I enrolled, there were 225 students. The preparatory class of 88 students was the largest in history at that time. During the academic years of 1952-53, we had only two professors with doctorate degrees, Dr. Powrie Doctor and Dr. Rosalyn Gardner.

Ron with roommates Robert Cheseny of Texas (left) and Truman Diot of New York (center) at College Hall in 1952.

In September 1952, seven CSD graduates—Connie Black, Alice Davenport, Corrine Lee, Robert Scribner, Julian Singleton, Constance Turner, and me—rode on sleeper trains from Berkeley to Washington, DC for three days. During a several-hour stopover in Chicago, Uncle Jack and Aunt Emy picked me up and graciously offered me a quick hot bath at their residence before taking me back to the station.

When we new students arrived at Kendall Green on the first day, we were sneered upon as lowly "rats" (a play on the word "prepaRATory") by scornful upperclassmen. We were ordered to do favors, but I was not affected at all. Once, an

HISTORICAL FACT:
GALLAUDET COLLEGE

In 1856, U.S. Postmaster General Amos Kendall donated two acres of his estate for a new school for deaf and blind pupils in Washington, DC. Edward Miner Gallaudet (EMG) was its first superintendent. One year later, U.S. Congress authorized the creation of the Columbia Institute for the Instruction of the Deaf, which was signed into law by President Abraham Lincoln. This became what is now Gallaudet University, the world's only liberal arts university for deaf students.

During the 1940s and 1950s, the late nineteenth century Collegiate Gothic brick and mortar College Hall housed administrative offices, a library, and a clinic on a first floor, along with an upperclassman dormitory on the second and third floors and a preparatory dormitory on the top floor. Shower facilities were in the basement; as a result, women were not allowed on the first floor after 5:00 p.m., when many of the males would descend to the basement naked, wrapped only in towels. Back then, no elevator existed. The three-story Fowler Hall served as a dormitory for women, and contained an indoor swimming pool in the basement. Classes were held at the nearby Lab Building and Dawes Hall. Socials and a college snack bar were held in the Tudor-style "Ole Jim," which now serves as an alumni office.

Since the Mason-Dixon line once symbolized a cultural boundary between the free North and the segregated South, the latter endured in its segregation practices until it was outlawed by the Civil Rights Act in 1964. Even though it was surrounded by segregated states, the District of Columbia, under control by U.S. Congress, remained free. The college was racially mixed; in contrast, the on-campus Kendall School for the Deaf was segregated until 1952.

upperclassman asked Robert Scribner whether I possessed skills in karate. He uttered "No," and the upperclassmen ganged upon me. I was the third Nikkei from CSD since 1922. At the time, only a very few Americans of Asian descent enrolled at Gallaudet College.

Ron was known to study well into the night under his desk lamp.

To alert roommates, a visitor "knocked" on the door by pulling a knob, releasing a chained iron weight that dropped and made the floor vibrate. The overhead lighting in the dorm rooms was automatically shut off at 10:00 p.m. and turned on at 6:00 a.m. Hallways and restrooms, as well as a reading room on the second floor, were illuminated all night.

In the fall of 1952, during icebreaker activities, prep students shared Deaf humor from all over the nation. The jokes were so popular that they lasted all night. Manual spellings and signs representing various states were often humorous but immodest, and many persist to this day.

I was assigned to Room 42 on the top floor of College Hall with two other preps: braggart Truman Diot (circa 1933-1988) from New York State and chain-smoking Robert Chesney (circa 1933-1998) from Texas. During the night, Truman peeked at me sleeping and later admitted that he had decided I was not gay. Apparently he had been misled to believe that one of two students from Japan was gay. Times were certainly different back then, not to mention that I was not from Japan.

Robert often complained about capitalism. Sure enough, sometime in the 1970s he was arrested in Los Angeles for fraud involving the Social Security Administration. He had made false claims using the legal names of famous authors such as

*Gallaudet College's 1952-53 preparatory class in front of Chapel Hall.
Ron is in the second row, third from right.*

Samuel Clemens (Mark Twain) and John Chaney (Jack London).
Over time, Truman and I could not tolerate Robert's stinky
smoking odor. We asked him to move out so we could find a
non-smoking roommate. He obliged, and he was replaced by
Robert Scribner.

When the lights in my dorm room automatically turned off
at 10:00 p.m., I moved to the perpetually illuminated hallway
to sit on the floor and resume studying. Sophomore Norman
Tsu of Shanghai, China, who worked as a busboy at a Chinese
restaurant, occasionally handed me a doggie bag. One night,
he delivered it to me as other students began gathering around
me, curious to see what was in the bag. When I opened it
exposing a fish tail, they quickly withdrew in disgust. That was
fine with me; this way I didn't have to share.

Truman and other classmates ridiculed me by saying
Chinese food was so terrible that even pigs refused to eat
it. I quickly countered and wagered with them. One Sunday
evening, I took them to the renowned Peking Cafe in the
exclusive Embassy Row in northwest district of Washington.
Before ordering, I asked them what they didn't like. Once
dishes were served, they indicated that the food still looked

disgusting. I told them to shut up and proceed. They cautiously began tasting, and they finally wolfed down all the food. Of course, I ordered them to pay up! Afterwards, they begged me to accompany them to a Chinese restaurant next time because they didn't know how to read the menu. We despised the cold cuts served every Sunday evening at the Gallaudet cafeteria due to fact that cooks didn't work then.

Ron and Alice Lougee in 1952.

Once, one classmate asked me how to speak "forty-two" for my room number. I mouthed it, and I was told it was indecent. Why? When I mouthed it, it looked as if I said "f--- you." As you see, I often fell for silly pranks, as did many others.

The following excerpt from an email Alice Lougee Hagemeyer recounts her recollection of our time at Gallaudet:

In the fall of 1952, I introduced myself to Ronald Hirano at the Gallaudet Chapel Hall during our preparatory year. I remember we were both shy with one another and I became infatuated with him. Ron was truly unique to me. He was completely different from any other boy I had dated prior to him. The best part of my preparatory year was having a new steady date—Ronald Hirano. I truly loved his company as I learned a lot from him.

While we dated, Ronald always talked about his educational values. He also always wanted to see me to be a professional and study well in school. He also shared his dream about our future success. He seemed to be worried sometimes about us dating, but he did not show it. His primary concern was about how other students would feel about me going with him because he was not white. In turn, I also noticed that he only dated women who were Asians before he met me and I was jealous of them and feared I would not match up to them.

After our preparatory year, when we returned home for the summer, we promised to write letters to one another. I always enjoyed reading his letters which were always filled with interesting news about life in San Francisco with people and events happening that were opposite to my life in my small hometown in rural western Nebraska. I spent most of my time painting and working on houses for my grandparents and others to earn money for my Gallaudet education. My widow mother did not have a phone and car, but she had a TV and of course TVs were not accessible in those years to the deaf. It was not until many years later that TVs came with the ability to caption shows. Truthfully, I do not remember what I wrote to Hirano that summer, but I assume that I talked about my summer job, my family and a few deaf friends who visited me from other towns. I remember I told them that my boyfriend was Japanese-American. I did not know what they thought about it in those years, but I recall that they were happy that I loved Gallaudet and made many new friends.

When I returned to Gallaudet in the fall as a freshman, I remember well that Ted, Hirano's roommate, began to pursue me and I did not want to date him. I did not know it until many years later after I married Ted that Hirano had a picture of his girlfriend back home in their room. I cannot remember why we did not stay together after that summer, but after our relationship ended, he dated my good friend, Toni and I began dating other boys. Although our time dating was at an end, Hirano was always and even today, in my heart. I have never forgot him over the years and I have been very grateful that today he and I still keep in touch with each other.

Wearing his trademark bow tie, Professor Edward Scouten taught a preparatory English class at eight o'clock in the mornings and worked as a counselor at the preparatory dormitory in the evenings. One morning, he noticed one of our classmates was absent. He told us to remain in class, and he went to the dormitory to search for the missing student. Several minutes later, he dragged the groggy, rumpled classmate back to class. Consequently, that dullard devised a rudimentary alarm system consisting of books placed on top of a net of parallel strings running around the top of his front and back bed frames, wound with a manual alarm clock nailed to the top of his dresser. When the

Edward Scouten was a legendary English professor at Gallaudet College.

alarm rang, it unwound and released the strings, dropping the books to wake him up.

In another incident, Professor Scouten gave us an assignment to recite thirty-two lines of Macbeth's "Dagger" speech as written by William Shakespeare for an examination the very next morning. We were warned that he earlier caught another student cheating with a small piece of typewritten paper attached to the interior of his jacket. Professor Scouten animatedly greeted us by manually spelling "GM" (good morning), "GA" (good afternoon), "GE" (good evening) and "GN" (good night). He was one of my favorite instructors.

As was college tradition for many years, students were hazed until a suspension of activities during the academic year of 1953-1954. The hazing resumed the next year. As was common at hearing colleges, we were hazed every weekend for a month or so. During class breaks, preparatory students were required to wear green caps inscribed with yellow letters, "RAT." Whenever we were asked for identification, we had to manually spell our full names, replacing each instance of the letter "i" with our middle finger. If we misspelled, upperclassmen grabbed and threw our caps away, continuously slapping at our bare heads until we recovered the caps.

After being forewarned, I taped a folded one-dollar bill to the sole of my right foot before bedtime. At two o'clock in the

59

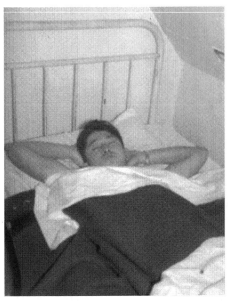

Ron asleep in his dorm room at Gallaudet's College Hall in 1952.

Ron as a college sophomore in 1955.

One of the activities preparatory students had to participate in was a "blind kissing" game, where females were blindfolded and tried to guess who kissed them.

The preparatory students put on a performance; Ron is at center.

Ron playfully poses with his Gallaudet classmates.
(L-R): Barbara Hanna, Virginia Luke, Connie Black,
and Alice Davenport.

morning, we were woken up by upperclassmen and led down to the basement. We were ordered to line up and take our clothes off. The upperclassmen then searched our clothes for hidden money. Being naked except for our underwear, we were forced to kneel. The hidden dollar bill partly peeled off my sweating foot. Behind me, another kneeling fellow recovered it and inserted it between my buttocks.

Preparatory students kneel as they are hazed by upperclassmen.

The upperclassmen commanded us to get dressed and then blindfolded us with bandannas. We formed a long line, placed our hands on the shoulders of the person in front of us, and hiked. At the end of the long march, we were separated and individually led to an assigned spot. We had to sit down and wait for ten minutes. After pulling the bandannas down from our eyes, we found ourselves sitting on marble grave markers in a huge cemetery. I immediately checked for the hidden bill in my butt, and it was gone. I walked to the gates at the cemetery entrance and found my classmates. We then hailed a cab back to Gallaudet.

One day, we defied orders from the upperclassmen. In retaliation, we were wakened overnight and marched to the basement. The upperclassmen punished us by making us apply automotive grease and lubricant all over our bodies. After that oily treatment, we hobbled to the showers for cleansing. I immediately ascended to my room to retrieve a large soap bar. For one hour or so, I repeatedly skimmed the grease off with a loose metal drain cover, and then scrubbed myself with the soap bar until I was completely cleansed. Other struggling preps, one by one, gave up. At breakfast, they wearily sat with greasy residue on their heads, while I was glisteningly clean.

I was grateful for this traditional Japanese cleansing custom.

On the morning of January 15, 1953, I was attending class when an instructor heard on the radio that there had been a train wreck at the nearby Union Station. After class, I quickly took a camera and walked there. I later read that an operator of the Pennsylvania Railroad train from New York City was not able to apply brakes as the train approached the station. He immediately radioed ahead to move all passengers to the rear cars, and warned people to clear out of the station. The locomotive crashed through the station lobby, but fortunately no one was injured nor killed.

Five days later, in the early hours of January 20, 1953, we strolled from the college to the east end of the National Mall, and stood there shivering for four hours to witness the presidential inauguration of Republican Dwight Eisenhower, ending the twenty-year Democratic dominance of Presidents Franklin D. Roosevelt and Harry Truman. Afterward, the parade lasted four more hours. It was such a historic event to witness.

CLASS OF 1957 LEGENDS

- **Ida Gray Hampton** (1933-present): First black female graduate of Gallaudet.
- **Gilbert Eastman** (1934-2006): Drama professor at Gallaudet, National Theatre of the Deaf actor, and co-host of the Emmy-winning *Deaf Mosaic* television show.
- **Betty Miller** (1934-2012): "Mother" of the De'VIA movement, Gallaudet art professor, co-founder of Spectrum, and authors of three books.
- **Alice Lougee Hagemeyer** (1933-present): Librarian, library activist, and one of fifteen Visionary Leaders honored during the Gallaudet University 150th anniversary celebration.

Texan classmate Donald Renick (circa 1933-1987) owned a secondhand Oldsmobile Eighty-Eight and he was notorious for reckless, high-speed driving. I was one of his favorites because of the German and Japanese Axis. He often refused requests from classmates for rides,

L-R: Gerald "Jerry" Pelarski, Ron, Donald Renick, Roger Pendergraft, and Ronald Jones at the Soviet Union Embassy in 1953.

so they would bypass him by asking me to help out.

During Easter break, Donald drove the Oldsmobile on a tour of New York and New England, accompanied by Truman Diot, Robert Scribner, and me. Just outside Washington, DC, Donald suddenly braked hard and the car skidded in a circle. Luckily, it did not hit anything. Still, Truman became so furious that he got out of the back seat and pushed Donald aside, taking over as driver.

Around midnight, we stopped at a station in New Jersey to refuel. Strolling around the parked car, I noticed that the car was missing both license plates. I notified Donald, and he asked an attendant to call his father in Corpus Christi, Texas, for help. After one or two hours of waiting, the father had not responded. So, I searched and found a carton in a trash can. I created a rudimentary blank license plate from the cardboard, writing on it based on Donald's driving document and posted it on the rear of the car. During the entire tour, none of the highway patrol nor police noticed that situation. Whew!

One spring day, Donald drove Jerry Pelarski, Roger Pendergraft, Ronald Jones, and me to visit the Soviet Union Embassy at 1125 Sixteenth Street Northwest. A member of its staff opened the front door and guided us through a long hallway between mirrored walls into a large lobby.

He then directed us upstairs to a cavernous ballroom, and we viewed huge landscape paintings, all dominated by Dictator Joseph Stalin. That incident was so prosaic that I left and hurried toward the front entry, followed by my friends. As I grasped the doorknob, I was shocked by electricity. The staff immediately shut it off and apologized to me.

Ron and Clarence Shimamura in 1952.

During my preparatory year, Clarence Shimamura (circa 1933-2000), the beautiful Nikkei daughter of a judge in Honolulu, Hawaii, quickly attracted curious men. As her popularity gradually deteriorated on campus, I gained courage to ask her on a date. She dressed luxuriously, and I took her to a restaurant. I became annoyed by her sumptuousness and almost went broke paying for dinner. During morning classes, Clarence often arrived late, joining me in the rear seating area. Her strong perfume almost overwhelmed me. She remained at school only one year.

Biology, taught by Professor Jonathan Hall, was a required course but not my favorite. I received a scalpel and an embalmed frog for dissection. I did not wait for instruction, and I quickly cut the carcass in half. Professor Hall halted me and told me not to chop it like a samurai. He gave me a replacement, and I obeyed his instructions.

One warm spring day, our class went to a picnic at Beaver Dam Pond, formerly a flooded quarry in Cockeysville, Maryland. A popular activity was to use a rope swing for jumping into the pond. At that time, the segregated park was for whites only. As we entered the park, we concealed a black classmate, Ida Gray, as we went through admissions.

In the spring of 1953, Professor Donald Padden (1921-2020), a 1945 Gallaudet graduate, selected ten of us to serve as guinea pigs in a research project for his graduate degree at the University of Maryland. He conducted the study at the Fowler Hall swimming pool at Gallaudet. In the first round, each of us sat on a stool on the end of a diving board, individually rotated several times, and then

Ron (front, far left) was a member of the Photo Club, selling his photographs.

were shoved off the board into the pool. The professor set a timer to record how long it took each of us to surface. In the next round, we were blindfolded and rubber caps put on our head, and the same process was repeated. The results were surprising. The late-deafened subjects wandered aimlessly underwater, unlike the congenitally deaf ones who quickly surfaced. In short, inner ear damage affected our navigation and surfacing skills.

Ron was a leading runner for Gallaudet.

During freshman and sophomore years, I photographed college activities and sports as a member of the Photo Club. I developed photos in a darkroom and then posted them on bulletin boards for sale. I made a decent profit.

Usually, I wore liberal, Californian-style attire. That attracted several classmates who dressed in conservative Eastern attire, so they asked me for a favor, which was buying

*Ron runs in a track meet
for Gallaudet.*

*Ron received the Low-Scorer
Award for cross country.*

*The 1953 Gallaudet cross country team;
Ron is in front at far left.*

Ron poses in a canoe on Potomac River in 1954. Behind him are the Lincoln Memorial and the Washington Monument.

Ron hangs the Class of 1957 banner, a tradition at the college, in "Ole Jim" (now the Peikoff Alumni House) as his fellow undergraduates cheer him on.

their attire. I obliged and made purchases when back home during summer break.

For three years, I participated in cross country, running in the 880-yard, one-mile and two-mile events. I trained daily, running fifty miles a week. On the junior varsity wrestling team, I competed in the 130-pound class. I was the first Asian athlete in intercollegiate sports at Gallaudet College. In 1953, I was asked to participate in five-thousand- and ten-thousand-meter races in the Seventh International Games for the Deaf, now the Deaflympics, in Brussels, Belgium, but I unfortunately was not able to go there due to funding difficulties.

During my freshman year, 1953-1954, I shared a second-floor corner dorm room in College Hall with my classmate Theodore "Ted" Hagemeyer (1931-2018) and senior Roger Johnson. This room was later converted to a museum and now adjoins the university president's office.

On October 15, 1954, Hurricane Hazel hit Washington, DC, reaching wind speeds up to ninety-eight miles per hour. After it passed, I went out to take photographs. Many trees on Kendall Green were toppled over, and portions of the roof were ripped off College Hall. That storm was the final one of the season.

In the fall of 1954, I leisurely browsed through the first annual college catalog. Gallaudet initially offered two degree programs after becoming accredited: Associate in Arts (AA) and Associate in Arts and Sciences (AAS). At that time, the college did not offer an engineering program that I wanted. I decided to pursue an associate degree and asked President Leonard Elstad (1899-1990) for an application. He asked me where I found out about the program and I pointed at the catalog. This catalog started a surge of applicants, but that popular shortcut was ultimately discontinued ten years later.

On June 4, 1955, Gallaudet College hosted its ninety-first commencement, and Delight Rice obtained an honorary doctorate degree in pedagogy. By a stroke of luck, I graduated with my associate degree in the same ceremony. President Elstad handed my degree to Delight, who in turn presented it to me. That unprecedented event was the first in Gallaudet College history.

COLLEGE BREAKS

During the 1952 fall break, Robert Scribner and I visited my uncle Hideo and my aunt Yoshi in New York City; Hideo was studying optometry at University of Columbia. They took us sightseeing in Manhattan. We climbed the steep, spiraling steps to the Statue of Liberty crown area; the torch was unfortunately closed to visitors.

During my 1952 Christmas vacation, I visited my favorite aunt Oshu Hirano in Chicago. She took me to Chicago Club of the Deaf and introduced me to Hannah Takagi. After socializing

Delight Rice (left) with Ron at Gallaudet's 91st commencement.

with other members, I chatted with A.L. Roberts, an elderly leader of the National Fraternal Society of the Deaf. Hannah's older sister Ruth graduated from CSD in 1940. In the spring of 1942, Hannah and Ruth were sent to the Manzanar Internment Camp at the foot of Sierra Nevada in Southern California. Afterwards, Hannah relocated to Chicago and attended Illinois School for the Deaf.

In the summer of 1953, Robert Scribner and I visited my uncle Fred and my aunt Toki in Cincinnati, Ohio. We did not sightsee because Aunt Toki was pregnant with Gordon Keith. However, they did drive us across the Ohio River to Covington, Kentucky, to dine at a fried chicken restaurant. That was a short time after the first of Kentucky Fried Chicken restaurants were franchised in 1952.

CHAPTER 6

Previous page:
Grandmother Ina Hirano's 100th Birthday Celebration in 1974; behind her is a portrait of her at a younger age.

CHAPTER 6
RETURNING HOME
(1955-1962)

In 1953, my family moved to a 1909 Craftsman style four-bedroom, two-bathroom, residence on 2816 Hillegass Avenue between Stuart Street and Russell Street in the Elmwood District of Berkeley, several blocks from CSD, which I had graduated from only a year before. Many CSD teachers and alumni resided in that neighborhood, such as the Pedersen family, the Amann family, and the Ladner family.

My father James converted the backyard into a beautiful Japanese-style garden with a small goldfish pool featuring a miniature waterfall and a lawn with Japanese maple trees, evergreen trees and tall bamboo, surrounded by Japanese-style fencing. He had a gardening helper and me dig up holes and plant the trees. This backbreaking work meant we had to replant the trees in different sites whenever he changed his mind. One morning, a raccoon was spotted grabbing and eating goldfish from the pool. James immediately called animal control to catch it.

In the late 1940s and early 1950s, about a dozen Chinese cabaret clubs thrived in Chinatown in San Francisco, catering to curious white males. Charlie Low's Forbidden City on 363 Sutter Street was an especially notable location for burlesque shows. James often partied at these clubs to the point of drunkenness. Whenever he was drunk, Bobby had to retrieve him and drive him home. He was occasionally caught driving drunk, and Bobby sometimes had to bail him out of jail.

The passage below is excerpted from an email my sister Carol sent me:

When I attended Willard Junior High School near our Hillegass residence in Berkeley, I asked you to teach me the ASL alphabet. You wanted to know about a basketball game that was on the radio. I drew a picture of the court with the baskets on both ends and made a list of the players on both teams. I interpreted the action play-by-play as I heard it on the radio. It was exhausting for me since basketball was such a fast-moving game and my signing was poor. I did a lot of pointing to the list of players. It was tough for me, but I managed to get through the game for you! I was happy you never asked me to do it again!

A lover of practical jokes, James occasionally faked a heart attack, frightening Bobby and me. Despite our scares, Bobby, Gordon, and I still pull pranks during family gatherings. This has earned us a reputation among our relatives and friends, who exclaim how devilish the Hirano men can be!

We often hosted guests for dinner at our residence, and my father would become so drunk that he repeatedly tried to pour whiskey into the guests' glasses, even when they refused. He often made offensive jokes, angering my mother and embarrassing my sisters.

James was once selected to be a part of cardiac research conducted by the nearby University of California, Berkeley. Participants in Japan, Hawaii, and California were evaluated on their nutrition and heart diseases. The results were interesting:

- *Japanese natives*: Lowest heart disease rate; diet consisted primarily of fish.
- *Japanese-Hawaiians*: Moderate heart disease rate; diet consisted primarily of fish and meat.
- *Japanese-Californians*: Highest heart disease rate; diet consisted primarily of meat.

I learned from my sisters that my father finally revealed the long-time secret of his father Hanakichi's mysterious early demise in 1920. It was syphilis, a deadly venereal disease, that he had become infected with when employed as a merchant marine. James and my siblings did not disclose this information to his surviving sisters Yone and Oshu and brother Jack, probably out of respect.

The Hirano Family in 1959. (L-R): Daniel, Janet, Grandma Ina, James, Mary, Carol, Bobby and Ron. Kneeling is Gordon with the family dog.

One day, Bobby drove me to school on his way to work in San Francisco. I was focused on reviewing my homework when I was abruptly thrown halfway through the front windshield as we crashed into a car ahead of us that had suddenly stopped. I was immediately sent to the hospital with a long cut across my forehead, which required stitches. That scar is still visible even though I applied olive oil to it daily per my mother's advice.

When I was a teenager, Bobby told me about my father's other family in Japan. I thought it was a joke at first. But one day, I noticed my mother crying after finding an intimate letter to my father from his mistress in Japan. Afterwards, I searched and found it in her bedroom drawer. I biked to Uncle Hachiro and Aunt Yone's house on Tremont Street in North Oakland and tried to show it to them, but they refused to read it. Some years later, our doorbell rang. When James opened the front door, there stood his mistress and a child. He quickly told Bobby to go upstairs to get money, which he gave to the woman. He then ordered Bobby to immediately drive them to a hotel in San Francisco. My distraught mother left for Los Angeles for a while.

An agent for a Hollywood movie production asked James to be an actor in the movie *The Ugly American*. He turned down the offer because he was preoccupied with his import business. My family was very much disappointed.

The below is from an email my sister Janet sent me:

Personally, I have very mixed emotions about being honest about our family. I have long known how our family was the subject of gossip when I was growing up and felt very ashamed that we were talked about behind closed doors or blatantly within earshot. Sometimes, when I was introduced to other people—some people would say, "Oh, you are from that Hirano family!" But, truthfully, I had no idea what was meant by that remark. But maybe going the route of telling the truth is the way to go.

James and Mary Hirano, Ron's parents, at Carol's wedding in 1968, which was held on their backyard deck.

Among the local Japanese community, the surname of Hirano is as common as Jones and Smith in other communities. In fact, my sister Carol didn't need to change her maiden name when she married David Hirano. Interestingly enough, I am the only Hirano in the American Deaf community as far as I know.

After the war, Hannah Takagi, the former CSD student who had relocated to Chicago, moved to Los Angeles and married Dwight Holmes, a Washington State School for the Deaf graduate. In the summer of 1959, I drove down to Los Angeles to visit them. They invited me for dinner in Chinatown with their friends, Iva DeMartini and her hearing husband. During dinner, one waiter vocally ridiculed us and imitated our signing. After dinner, Iva's husband complained to the manager about the waiter, and the waiter was fired on the spot. Later, the widowed Iva committed suicide by jumping from her upper apartment at the Pilgrim Tower, where Deaf seniors resided.

I once asked Uncle Hachiro for a drafting job at his architectural office in Oakland, but my request was apparently overruled by Aunt Yone. While complaining about his slow, fluctuating business, Hachiro repeatedly asked me how well my drafting employment was doing. Every time, I replied, "I am doing well." Thank goodness I worked for a medium-sized architectural products fabricating firm, not an architect's smallish office.

ADDITIONAL STUDIES AFTER GALLAUDET

After graduation from Gallaudet College in 1955, I enrolled at Heald College. On the upper floor of the Van Ness Street office building, I took mechanical drawing and architecture.

HISTORICAL FACT:
HEALD COLLEGE & CITY COLLEGE OF SAN FRANCISCO

Established in 1863, Heald College was a private business college in San Francisco. It grew to encompass several campuses in California, Oregon, and Hawaii. It was eventually taken over by a for-profit education company called Corinthian Colleges. Heald closed its doors for good when, in 2015, Corinthian was forced to shutter all their campuses by the U.S. Department of Education due to misrepresentation.

Founded in 1935, the City College of San Francisco, the largest two-year community college in California, serves thirty-five thousand students at eleven campuses over the city. It now offers free tuition exclusively for city residents.

After being briefly employed, I attended City College of San Francisco I majored in architecture, but I was forced to take several required courses as well, such as political science. Since I could not find a willing notetaker during a political science class, I read the textbook during the lectures. The strict professor ordered me to stop reading and asked me to lipread. I told him that I could not do that, and he left me alone. Eventually, I dropped the class.

POST-COLLEGE EMPLOYMENT

After struggling in architectural studies for two years, I finally landed my first full-time drafting job in 1957 at Metalco through a kind, Deaf widow Olive E. Seely (1900-1996). Her husband Perry E. Seely (1886-1949) was the founding father of California School for the Deaf in Riverside and also the president of California Association of the Deaf in 1937. Olive's hearing nephew Ricky Small, who could sign, trained me in drafting work for a brief time before he left.

Metalco, now closed, was established in 1946 in the small industrial city of Emeryville squeezed between Berkeley to the north and Oakland to the east and south. Its minuscule business specialized in aluminum anodizing and grinding. My initial project was an aluminum storefront frame for a small store on Telegraph Avenue in Berkeley. I was bothered by a grandfatherly co-worker's eccentric behavior as well as toxic dust from metal grinding and polishing next door, so I quit after one year.

After a short job search in 1958, I was interviewed by a kind, friendly drafting supervisor, Walter Oertel at Soulé Steel Company. In 1911, Edward Soulé founded the steel company in San Francisco, pioneering steel rebars. It flourished and expanded to nine fabrication shops, a steel mill, a steel building division and an architectural building products division. Later, the company relocated to Los Angeles, and, in 1983, converted to Soulé Software, selling programs for the rebar market.

My interview was interpreted by an office employee, Sylvan Selig, who had Deaf parents. Sylvan's Deaf father Isdore Selig was one of the early leaders of San Francisco Club of the Deaf (now the San Francisco Deaf Club). I was hired on the spot.

Ron worked at the Soulé Steel Company in San Francisco for 15 years.

I worked with fifteen colleagues in a large drafting department for the division of Soulé Architectural Building Products, fabricating and installing aluminum windows, window walls, and curtain walls for commercial buildings and skyscrapers. At work, I communicated through pencil and paper. The son of the founder, Vice-President Stanley Soulé, occasionally greeted me at work; he typically did not greet other coworkers.

Checking a peer's shop drawings, I once foresaw a possible gap in the exterior construction and pointed it out to him. He stubbornly disagreed. To challenge him, I found, cut up, and taped together discarded cardboard, building a small-scale mock-up based on the drawings. Ultimately, I proved him wrong. To this day, I firmly believe that Deaf people have superior visualization skills compared to hearing people.

I taught one of my office colleagues basic sign language, including all the swear words. My obscene signs spread throughout the office and my coworkers quickly picked them up. I was sometimes made fun of by one or two other peers because I was Deaf, but I was often able to discern their facial and body language and quickly silence them. I even used an interoffice phone to vocally swear at them, watching their reactions through their windows. I also once put pencil shavings into a coworker's closed umbrella, and when he opened it, the shavings fluttered all over him.

A deaf welder, Timothy Beyer, worked in the fabricating shop. We occasionally visited each other in our departments. He was a graduate of the Ohio School for the Deaf and a member of the Gallaudet class of 1968. After Soulé closed, we lost contact with each other. Forty-two years later, I received a surprising letter from him in Alabama. We then chatted with each other through videophone.

One day, my Gallaudet classmate Donald Renick visited me at work. When he vocally chatted with one of my peers, my coworkers craned their necks out of their work cells to locate who was speaking. That made me very uncomfortable. Donald was educated at the Central Institute for the Deaf in St. Louis, which promotes speech and lipreading and strictly prohibits sign language. I believe poorly trained people with weak speech cause much more irritation than written communication or ASL.

In my fifteen years at Soulé, I was a junior draftsman, a senior draftsman, and then a project engineer. When the division closed in the fall of 1973, I received a generous severance check.

CHAPTER 7

Previous page:
Ron and Kay enjoy the sun from the beach of their family property in Anchor Bay, California.

CHAPTER 7
MARRIAGE
(1962-PRESENT)

Have you noticed many unmarried Deaf Nikkei elders? One reason is that during the early twentieth century their parents would disown them if they dated or married outside of their culture. My parents wanted me to find a Deaf bride from Japan. I rejected their request because I preferred Americans; after all, I was one. Following Japanese tradition in the United States, members of families generally intermarried until the 1950s and 1960s. I was so fortunate that my parents accepted my non-Japanese bride-to-be, breaking with that cultural norm.

Another common misconception is that Chinese and Japanese cultures are similar. They are not. Chinese students regularly attend public schools during the weekdays, and are mandated to study the Chinese language on Saturdays. In contrast, Japanese is voluntary for Nikkei students. In other words, Chinese people cherish their language while Nikkei people generally do not care about Japanese.

In 1960, Stan Smith and I attended the International Catholic Deaf Association conference at Whitcomb Hotel in San Francisco. There, I met Catherine "Kay" Farkas from Milwaukee and asked her out on a date. She accepted. Stan accompanied me as I took her out for dinner at a restaurant in Chinatown. In 1961, I drove a Volkswagen Beetle with my thirteen-year-old brother Gordon from California to Chicago, stopping at Uncle Jack and Aunt Emy's house for a night. Leaving Gordon there, I drove ninety miles north to Milwaukee. Upon arrival at Kay's house, I was overwhelmed by her curious

HISTORICAL FACT:
REDRESS AND REPARATIONS FOR INCARCERATION

Inspired by the American civil rights movement, Japanese-Americans launched a campaign for redress in 1978. Two years later, Congress created a commission on redress and reparations. On February 24, 1983, the commission issued a report condemning the internment as unjust and motivated by racism and xenophobia rather than military necessity. The Civil Liberties Acts of 1988 and 1992 respectively signed by Ronald Reagan and George H.W. Bush paid a tax-free reparation of $20,000 to each of the 60,000 surviving internees.

Hannah Takagi Holmes, the Deaf Nikkei who relocated to Illinois, was so bitter about her incarceration experience that she feverishly advocated for reparations for internees for years. She testified during televised Congressional hearings with interpreters, and was featured in the nation's leading Japanese-American daily newspaper *Rafu Shimpo* in Los Angeles. She urged me to convince my parents and relatives, but they retained *shikata ga nai*. I refused to apply for reparation because I was never interned. Even so, my siblings persuaded me to apply, and I finally yielded.

mother and aunts. Eventually, they accepted me as a future part of their family. Ironically, Kay's father Anton's birthday was on December 7, the day of the 1941 Pearl Harbor attack.

In 1961, as Kay disembarked the plane outside at Oakland Airport, she looked up at the terminal and was caught off-guard when she saw my parents and siblings looking at her. They were on the upper terminal level, excitedly awaiting her arrival. My father very much enjoyed speaking with her. In Berkeley, I introduced Kay to my local friends and later took her for a tour in San Francisco. Later, my mother asked me why I did not choose a college-educated girl since Kay was a high school graduate. Displeased, I responded that she herself was a high school graduate.

Newlyweds Ron and Kay Hirano during Christmas 1962.

On June 16, 1962, our wedding was conducted by Father Lawrence Murphy at a Roman Catholic church in Milwaukee. My parents and my siblings attended, except my youngest brother Gordon, who graduated from Berkeley High School on the same day.

For twenty-four years, the late Father Murphy was the director of St. John's School for the Deaf in Milwaukee, established in 1876. He left in 1974, largely in an attempt to cover up a notorious sexual abuse scandal where he molested two hundred boys. The scandal was eventually featured in a documentary for HBO. The school was ultimately closed in 1983. Former students filed four lawsuits against the Archdiocese of Milwaukee, and they later received reparations.

During our honeymoon, we drove to Seattle for the World's Fair. One early evening, we stopped at a gas station on the outskirts of the small town of Worthington in southwestern Minnesota. After filling up, I asked an attendant for recommendation of a restaurant in town. As we dined there, unexpectedly, the attendant entered the restaurant, found us, and handed me my credit card I had left at the gas station. Talk about Midwestern courtesy!

We stopped at the Badlands National Monument, now a national park, in South Dakota, After taking numerous pictures, I wondered why my Nikon camera did not run out of film. I opened the camera and found it empty. At the Seattle

fair, we did not
see any Deaf
locals, but we
met two Deaf
couples from
California,
Warren and
Ann Jones of
Fremont and
Sheldon and
Mary McArtor of
San Francisco.

Ron's parents, James and Mary Hirano, circa 1975.

In July,
my parents
hosted a post-wedding reception in
their Japanese garden at our house
in Berkeley. As our guests mingled,
lawn sprinklers suddenly sprayed,
scattering the guests. James rushed to
turn off the automatic sprinklers and,
embarrassed, apologized to the slightly
wet guests. They still reminisce to this
day about that mishap.

Ina Hirano

In the early 1960s, my parents
drove along the breathtaking
Mendocino coast, one hundred miles
north of San Francisco, in search of a potential property. That
was long before the distinctive Sea Ranch was developed. In
1963, they finally purchased a coastal property near Anchor
Bay consisting of 1.87 acres with one-hundred-yard-long
beach. In 1986, our family partnership bought a second 1.7-
acre lot adjacent to the original one. The properties are fully
forested with a 125-foot-high bluff with a precipitous trail with
a rope down to the shore. Family members and friends still
camp, fish, and swim there to this day. The new redwood stairs
down to the beach were constructed by our nephew Matthew
Matsuoka and his contractors. The stairs allows us elderly
siblings to have access to the water.

Three generations of the Hirano family gather in 2015
at Kelly Hirano's residence. Ron is in the very back, third from right.

Ina, my father's mother, died at the age of 106 in 1981. My father James died three years later at the age of 80. My mother died at the age of 91 in 2000. Even with the passing of our parents and grandmother, my siblings and I maintain our tight-knit family. We periodically hold gatherings for three generations of the family, consisting of twenty-five Sansei, Yonsei, and Gosei. The best part is my brother Daniel and his wife Colleen have taken ASL classes, and he has been instrumental in organizing our monthly sibling gatherings, including ASL classes. During the COVID-19 pandemic, our meetings went virtual.

From 1962 to 1965, Kay and I rented small, humble one-bedroom apartments in San Bruno and Oakland. The first visitor was my Gallaudet classmate Virginia Luke of Washington State. In 1965, my aunt Masae Sato, who was the manager of an apartment building in San Francisco, offered us a place. We relocated across the bay to a larger apartment at 2135 California Street, owned by the Morioka family for years. James did not approve of the move because he quarreled with the Morioka siblings over the ownership and management of the eight-unit apartment building. I believe he attempted to

Ron on one of the family's frequent trips to the beach, circa 1975.

Ron and his mother Mary, circa 1985.

The Hirano siblings in 2015. Back (L-R): Daniel, Ron, Bobby and Carol; Front (L-R): Janet and Gordon.

dominate that business. Eventually, my brother Daniel and his wife Colleen rented that apartment.

After nine years of renting, I finally recognized that home ownership was a good investment. In the spring of 1971, the fluctuating mortgage interest rate dipped to its lowest level in several years. At that time, we needed to make a twenty percent down payment. We asked my father for a loan and he refused. We ended up selling our stocks at a loss. We began to seek a home in San Francisco. My drafting colleague recommended the Miraloma Park neighborhood, sited between Twin Peaks to the north and City College of San Francisco to the south, on the southeastern slope of the 927-foot high Mount Davidson.

After a long search, we finally found a two-story house with three bedrooms, one-and-a-half bathrooms, and a single-car garage. The house had a breathtakingly panoramic "million-dollar" view overlooking the southern part of the city, from the bay in the east to the ocean in the west. It was so appealing that we competed intensely against two bidders, and eventually won. That purchase happened three years before the opening of the Glen Park BART Station, only a few blocks downhill. The residence is also a half-block walk from the Muni bus stop and only several blocks from Freeway 280. My research and persistence certainly paid off!

EMPLOYMENT

Briefly employed at another firm near the site of Soulé, I received a job offer from James Bedford, the former vice president of Soulé Architectural Building Products who was now president of Gavin Company. I was interviewed and hired on the spot, joining my former Soulé coworker Dennis.

After several years, I complained to Bedford about being ignored because my peers were promoted but I was not. He eventually called me for a meeting with an interpreter, and offered me a new position of project manager, which I immediately accepted. A young hearing ASL-literate trainee was hired, and I trained him in drafting work. I oversaw several draftspeople. Consequently, I was often assigned complex projects unlike my colleagues' simple ones. However, I did not whine.

One day, I flew down to Los Angeles for a troubleshooting task. I met the company vice president Bud

Ron stands in front of the Fireman's Fund Insurance Company headquarters in Novato, California.

and contractors at the construction site downtown. When we entered the temporary construction elevator, an operator spoke to me. I answered by pointing to my ear. In response, he displayed his middle finger to me, which angered me. The people there laughed at me even more. It was one of my worst and most degrading experiences.

Another time, I was assigned a large project, Fireman's Fund Insurance Company headquarters in Novato, north of San Francisco. I was given a schedule of one year. Due to a complex, asymmetrical building design, I warned the president that it would be impossible to complete the project on time. He ignored the warning. Sure enough, the project took three years, causing a financial loss.

Another time, I drove with an interpreter to the Fireman's Fund job site for troubleshooting. I inspected the facility and found the edge of the concrete floor slab out of line for anchoring curtain walls. The concrete contractor failed to adhere to my specifications, so he had to perform costly, tedious slab cutting at his own expense.

President Bedford, an interpreter, and I attended a meeting with a general contractor, an architect, and a construction manager in San Francisco. The main discussion focused on the variance in the olive-colored anodizing of

aluminum panels for the Fireman's Fund project. To resolve
that situation, I recommended that the panels be painted
for color consistency, but the architect overruled me.
Eventually, the anodized color of the panels looked so terribly
inconsistent that they had to be painted over. The headquarter
was abandoned for seven years before being sold to a housing
developer in January 2021.

After the Gavin Company went out of business, I became
employed at another firm in Oakland and quit after one
year. After mailing out twenty resumes, I was interviewed
by two small firms, but their interviewers were skeptical of
my twenty-year drafting experience because I was Deaf. My
former Soulé colleague Harry was hired by Blakeway Metal
Works. The century-old Blakeway Metal Works started as a
small fabricator of aluminum architectural products in San
Francisco. It was later bought by a German native who worked
there, John Uth. When the business flourished, an additional
draftsperson was needed so Harry recommended me, and I
began my employment with Blakeway Metal Works.

According to a corporate tradition, whenever business
declines, the last employee hired generally gets laid off first.
When business slowed at Blakeway, I thought I would lose
my job. Instead, Harry's employment was terminated. This
showed me that my employer had finally acknowledged how
well I performed.

I was assigned to design aluminum ornamental trims for
a canopy above the front entrance of Sheraton Palace Hotel in
San Francisco. My installers were not able to put the trims in
place because a steel frame was constructed out of tolerance.
The contractor had failed to follow my specifications.
Therefore, his crew had to uninstall, rework, and reinstall the
frame at his expense.

I also had one of the most challenging projects in
my career. This job consisted of two aluminum circular
ornamental trims with grilles, one of which was to be
installed on a canopy above the corner entrance, and the
other at the top roof level of the 88 Kearny Street skyscraper
in downtown San Francisco. Four sets of long aluminum

trim extrusions and sheet strips were transported to the Los Angeles bending facility, and the bending process was based on my calculations and specifications. Two additional sets were backups in case of fabrication discrepancy. The trims were fabricated and installed without a hitch. I considered it one of my masterpieces.

Monthly company investment reports were distributed among employees. I occasionally inspected and discussed my drawings with shop workers. One day, one of the shop workers showed me one of the reports. I read it, pinched my nose, and gestured thumbs down to him. Later, President Uth came to my office. He offered me the opportunity to serve on a corporate investment committee with an interpreter, and I immediately accepted.

Twice, I was summoned to jury duty. San Francisco law required Deaf individuals be allowed to serve on a jury and be provided with sign language interpreters. Uth himself once asked me for advice on how to evade a jury duty summon, but did not succeed.

I received a job offer from the former Soulé drafting manager, Walter Oertel, who was employed at Forderer Cornice Works. I declined because of my demanding work. Blakeway eventually went out of business due to the September 11th attacks.

In 1993, I decided to leave Blakeway because of its slow business. I soon landed a drafting job at Forderer with a recommendation from my former Soulé supervisor Walter Oertel. Forderer Cornice Works, founded by a German immigrant in 1875 in San Francisco, manufactured and distributed security and detention metal hollow doors and frames. It is now located in Hayward, thirty miles south San Francisco. I found my work there pretty routine. However, I was assigned a special project for a guard watch tower inside a new jail addition at the San Francisco Hall of Justice. It was challenging due to its asymmetrical shape. The vice president was impressed with my work, which I consider my final drafting masterpiece.

In late 1995, my manual drafting work became obsolete because of a new drafting technology, computer-aided design (CAD). I was eventually replaced by a low-paid technician. I was, thus, ready for retirement. Sayonara!

Ron (in front with his dog) takes his group on a backpacking trek in a wilderness area near Lake Tahoe, California.

A NEW CAREER IN EDUCATION

Founded in 1965, Ohlone College, a community college, serves the twin cities of Fremont and Newark. It is named after the local Native American tribe and is three miles south of CSD. Since 1972, the Center for Deaf Studies at Ohlone College has served up to two hundred students every year. Its first dean was George Attletweed (1930-1991), a graduate of CSD and San Francisco State University.

In 1977, I was asked by Ohlone College's Center for Deaf Studies to become a part-time instructor for a backpacking course. I taught fifteen backpackers, training them for a weekend trek in the High Sierra. I later taught technical math and ASL.

Three years later, the infamous State Proposition 13 was passed, which significantly reduced property taxes supporting schools and colleges, and my employment was terminated. The effects of Proposition 13 are still felt to this day.

In the late summer of 1982, I began a new job at SouthWest Collegiate Institute for the Deaf (SWCID) in Big Spring, Texas, as a drafting and design technology program instructor. SWCID was established on November 6, 1979, by the Howard County Junior College District board in Big Spring, Texas. Its founding father and first executive director was Dr. Douglas J.N. Burke (1931-1988), a 1955 Gallaudet graduate. The first classes started in November 1980, and today the program continues to serve as many as 125 students who range in age from twenty to thirty years.

My class consisted of twelve students, including three Iranian immigrants. When I assigned them homework due the next day, many of them did not complete it. I asked them why, and they told me they spent time with their girlfriends in the dormitory. I asked, "Does that help you to find a job?" and they replied no. I told them to focus on their studies on weeknights and spend time on the weekends with their girlfriends.

The 1979-81 American-Iranian hostage crisis had created hostility toward the Iranian students at SWCID, and they asked me for help. I calmed them down and told them they were so fortunate that they were not imprisoned in concentration camps like Japanese-American citizens during World War II.

For a couple of years, I sent numerous memos asking Dean Bernard Jones to offer more technical courses rather than academic ones since academic courses were available at Gallaudet University and National Technical Institute of the Deaf. Also, a majority of students at SWCID were vocationally oriented. My numerous requests were denied. After two frustrating years, I decided to resign. The timing was perfect because Gavin Company asked me to return.

CHAPTER 8

Previous page:
Ron and Kay stand in front of a statue of Delight Rice at Philippine School for the Deaf in 2017.

96

CHAPTER 8
SIDE BUSINESSES (1966-PRESENT)

Althodugh my career was both in engineering and then teaching, I also was involved with numerous side businesses that took me in many innovative directions.

STOCK MARKET

By reading books and newspapers, I taught myself about investing in mutual funds and later the stock market. I encouraged my father to invest in the stock market, and since he had a significant income from his import business, he became a successful investor in American and Japanese stocks. Due to my limited income, I did not do as well.

BACKPACKING AND MOUNTAINEERING

One day, my colleague at Soulé Steel suggested that I join a Sierra Club backpacking group. I participated in several summer and winter backpacking and mountaineering treks, learning plenty of skills. My hearing backpacking friends, Phil and Rita Nowlin, encouraged

Ron and Kay on one of their backpacking trips.

me to join the California Alpine Club, which owned two clubhouses at the foot of Mount Tamalpais and Echo Summit near Lake Tahoe. We backpacked with them through Desolation Wilderness from Echo Summit.

Ron, in front at right, climbed to the summit of Half Dome in Yosemite circa 1975.

In 1966, I started a side business guiding backpacking and mountaineering treks as an alpine guide. For sixteen years, I led numerous summer and winter treks with Deaf and hearing groups of twelve or fewer. I also guided them in climbing various summits along High Sierra. CSD and Gallaudet alumni Donald Bullock, Kenneth Norton, Alyce and Gilmer Lentz, Ella Lentz, and Virginia Luke were part of the treks.

INCOME TAX SERVICE

One day in 1984, a family meeting was held at my mother's Hillegass Street residence in Berkeley. With an interpreter, we siblings discussed our late father's tax issue; he owed a large sum of taxes to the Internal Revenue Service. My sister Carol suggested that my mother, Mary, assign me as the caretaker of that problem because I was the eldest sibling, in line with Japanese custom. I accepted, and spent weekends sorting out documents at the San Francisco business office and the Berkeley residence; my mother paid me for my work. I then obtained power of attorney and I contacted the Oakland IRS office for an appointment with an interpreter. I went to the office, and I met a friendly tax inspector. She informed me that an interpreter was not available. I asked the inspector if we could proceed with pen and paper, and she agreed. During the examination process, I handed each document to her, which she then checked on her computer. Next, she accepted it as evidence, and deducted it from the debt. As a result, the debt was reduced by ninety percent! My mother and my siblings were elated, as was I.

My mother then designated me as a trustee for the family finances. Checking on her finances, I found out that my parents had provided loans to my siblings for down payments on the purchase of houses—although my father had refused my request—but I remained silent. My mother eventually told me how sorry my father was for denying my request for a loan. My brother Daniel was then appointed as a co-trustee to communicate with the lawyer and certified public accountant.

I eventually attended an evening tax class at the downtown campus of San Francisco State University. I obtained a tax preparer certificate, passed an examination for a state license, and started an income tax service called The Tax Signs in 1985. The side business flourished for nineteen years, serving more than four hundred Deaf and hearing clients. In 2004, I discontinued the business to focus on chairing the 2005 Deaf Seniors of America (DSA) national conference.

WRITING AND DESIGNING A BOOK

For over fifteen years, I wrote, edited and designed numerous newsletters, including the Bay Area Coalition of Deaf Senior Citizens newsletter *Senior Quest*, the CSD Class of 1952 newsletter *1952 Eagles*, and the CSD Alumni Association newsletter *The Alumni Eagle*. My experience helped me write several books. At the urging of my friends and siblings, I authored and designed my first book *The Life Story of Mother Delight Rice and Her Children*. It is a biography of my foster mother, Delight Rice, who established the first permanent Deaf

The Life Story of
Mother Delight Rice
and Her Children
The First Teacher of the Deaf in the Philippines

RONALD M. HIRANO

school in the Philippines in 1907. She was the hearing daughter of Deaf parents who graduated from Ohio School for the Deaf.

I spent five years researching and two years writing and designing the book. My manuscript was edited by Trudy Suggs, the owner of T.S. Writing Services. When the editing was completed, I planned to find a publisher. By coincidence, Trudy had established an independent publishing company, Savory Words Publishing, specializing in Deaf authors. When discussing publishing options with her, she asked me to serve as a guinea pig for her new company and I accepted that challenge. After about one year, my first book was published in 2014, and served as the launching pad for several other books through her company.

Ron signing books at DLS-CSB-SDEAS in Manila in 2015.

In August 2014, copies of the book were shipped to Manila in the Philippines for distribution. The book stirred much exhilaration among Deaf schools and the Deaf community. In fact, Febe Sevilla, a staff interpreter at De La Salle-College of Saint Benilde, School of Deaf Education and Applied Studies (DLS-CSB-SDEAS), said about the book, "I just found the Holy Grail of Filipino Deaf history."

In January 2015, Kay and I flew to the Philippines for a two-week book tour. Upon arrival in Manila, we were stunned finding ourselves feeling like instant celebrities at Deaf schools and colleges. I gave the following series of presentations:

- On January 31, the Philippine School for the Deaf Alumni Affairs Association invited me for a book presentation before two hundred alumni.

Ron and Kay surrounded by
Philippines School for the Deaf students in 2015.

- On February 3, I gave a lecture at Philippine School for the Deaf attended by nine hundred students, educators and officials. I presented books to officials of the Department of Education (DepEd). DepEd is an executive department of the national government subject to presidential election.
- On February 4-5, I gave speeches before several groups of students and staff totaling two hundred at DLS-CSB-SDEAS promoting Filipino Sign Language. My ASL was interpreted into Filipino Sign Language by Rafael "Rafy" Domingo, a doctoral student at Gallaudet. I gave five copies of my book to the DLS-CSB-SDEAS library.
- At the administrative offices of the 8,600-student DLS-CSB, I formally presented my books to President Brother Dennis Magbanua and Chancellor Robert Tang.
- On February 9, I lectured before sixty students and staff at CAP College for the Deaf (the oldest college for Deaf students in the Philippines), which teaches its courses in ASL. I donated two books to its library.

Kay and Ron pose in front of a statue at the Philippines School for the Deaf honoring Delight Rice.

Two years later, at the end of November 2017, Kay and I flew back to Manila for the unveiling ceremony of a bronze sculpture of Mother Delight Rice sitting on a chair and embracing a Deaf girl and a blind boy. The ceremony took place on Monday, December 4, 2017, on the front campus of the Philippine School for the Deaf, attended by the mayor of Pasay City, officials, administrators, faculty, staff, and students. The cost of the statue and base was defrayed by book earnings and donations. It was later proclaimed a national historic landmark.

Ron gives a talk about his book at PSD.

Ron signs books at PSD.

(L-R): Interpreter Jun Sevilla, Ron, Kay and Officer-in-Chief Lovelyn G. Bacera in front of the PSD building.

CHAPTER 9

Previous page:
The 2005 Deaf Seniors of America conference in San Francisco brought one of the organization's largest-ever attendance, with over 2,300 registered participants.

CHAPTER 9
COMMUNITY SERVICE

I have always valued community service because I believe volunteerism is mentally and physically healthy, and it potentially extends longevity. My mottoes were and are: *Making a mistake is my teacher*, and *Who is your boss? Your body, not your brain!*

BAY AREA ASIAN DEAF ASSOCIATION

During the 1990s, I served as an advisor to the Bay Area Asian Deaf Association board. The board meetings were often disorderly because of infighting among immigrant members. Those disturbing incidents persisted to the point of animosity among Deaf schools and communities in Asia. I repeatedly tried to appease the quarreling board members by trying to have them separate personal matters from business, to no avail. I gave up after some time. I am happy to report that the organization has gradually matured and its membership is much more diverse nowadays with positive interactions.

BAY AREA COALITION OF DEAF SENIOR CITIZENS

When the Bay Area Coalition of Deaf Senior Citizens (BACDSC) was formed in 1995, my CSD classmate Julian "Buddy" Singleton was elected as its first president while I was its first treasurer. For fifteen years, I successively ascended from that position to second vice president and then president.

Ron calls to order a meeting of the Bay Area Coalition of Deaf Senior Citizens in 2008 with Elizabeth Kolombatovic.

I was the editor of the organization's *Senior Quest* newsletter for six years. In 1999, the organization clinched the bid for the 2005 Deaf Seniors of America national conference.

Bay Area Coalition of Deaf Senior Citizens officers. Back (L-R): Daniel Lynch and Larry Obray. Front (L-R): Ron, Buddy Singleton, and Elizabeth Kolombatovic.

DEAF SENIORS OF AMERICA

In 1997, I was unanimously elected as the Deaf Seniors of America (DSA) board treasurer at its fourth biennial conference in Phoenix, the only Asian on the all-white board. I was immediately deluged by white conference attendees who wanted to extend my term beyond the limit of three terms (of two years each); I regretfully had to decline. Two years later, I was elected the 2005 DSA conference chair at a BACDSC general meeting. After six years of planning, negotiation, bidding, and delegating, the conference in San Francisco drew more than 2,300 attendees, one of the largest in DSA's history. It was a great time that is still remembered by many today.

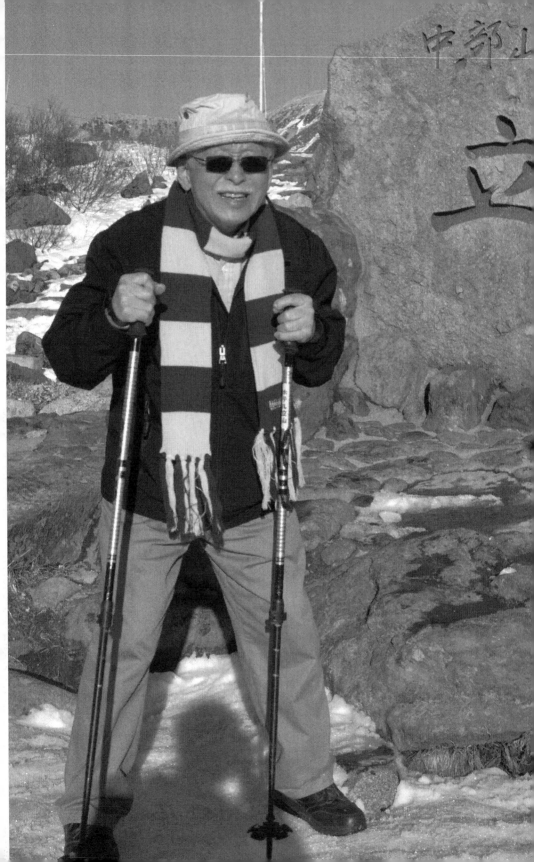

Previous pages:
Ron and Kay at Tateyama in the Japan Alps in 2018.

112

CHAPTER 10
SELECTED TRAVELS

Another passion I have is traveling the world with my wife. It is a joy to meet Deaf people in other countries and to learn about each area's culture, ways, and traditions. I have been fortunate to travel so much, both for pleasure and business.

NEW ZEALAND

As Australia, Canada and New Zealand are Dominions of British Commonwealth, their residents speak English. Deaf Australians and New Zealanders use British Sign Language, which

Ron and Kay take in the view at Mount Cook National Park, New Zealand, in 2000.

differs from American Sign Language (ASL); with British Sign Language, two hands are used for the manual alphabet while in America, one hand is used. Interestingly enough, Canadians use ASL, although some also use Quebecois Sign Language.

In December 1988, Kay and I flew down to New Zealand for the quadrennial Deaflympics at Christchurch. After the overnight flight, we arrived at the small Auckland International Airport, surrounded by farms with cows. Life was laid back there; this was before tourism became popular as a result of the *The Lord of the Rings* trilogy being filmed there. Moreover, we visited during New Zealand's summer, when it was winter in the United States. Everyone celebrated Christmas Day and New Year's Day outdoors at the beaches and parks. Trees and flowers were blooming everywhere, and nearby farms were harvesting crops.

On New Year's Eve, we hailed a taxi to drive us to Auckland Deaf Society's two-story clubhouse. We found ourselves the only American visitors and struggled to converse in our rudimentary BSL. The president of the club graciously introduced us to people, who were all friendly, and handed us two sets of coasters illustrated with images of the clubhouse. We also befriended an elderly lady, Ann d'Este, who worked at the club as a volunteer; she regularly corresponded with us up until a few years ago, when the letters stopped coming for unknown reasons.

North Island is one of the two main islands in New Zealand. One of its largest industries is forest products. We were impressed by the efficient system of planting, growing, and cutting huge Douglas Fir trees, based on a ten- to forty-year rotation. The lumber is chiefly imported to Japan. We also stopped and lodged at the seaside art deco city of Napier and the hot spring resort town of Rotorua, where we attended a sheep exhibition and met up with my college mates Richard and Bonnie Caswell of Maryland. After driving southward, we arrived at the capital city of Wellington, which we found to resemble San Francisco. The prevailing winds came northward from Antarctica.

Departing Wellington, we flew down to Christchurch on the coast of South Island by the South Pacific Ocean. We attended the opening ceremony of the Deaflympics, where we surprisingly encountered another Gallaudet classmate Jack Hathway (1930-2012) and his wife Marie Ann of Wisconsin. We spent a few days watching various sports and then spent two weeks driving around the enchanted island, topped by the majestic Southern Alps. We returned and enjoyed the closing days at the games. We met other American spectators, who "wasted" two entire weeks at the competitions, and told them how much they had missed by not touring the beautiful island.

JAPAN

Kay and I flew to Tokyo, Japan, for the 11th Congress of the World Federation of the Deaf (WFD) on July 2-11, 1991. This was the first time it was held outside of Europe or the United States, and it drew more than seven thousand attendees, the largest in history, including 1,063 oversea conferees from 52 nations. The WFD president was Yerker Andersson, Ph.D., (1929-2016), a popular Gallaudet professor who was a naturalized American from Sweden.

Meri Hirose and Peggy Prosser in October 2018.

As a Deaf American native, I experienced a slight cultural shock in how I differed from Deaf Japanese natives. I observed that they were highly educated and sophisticated; their occupations were largely in business and industrial professions such as independent architecture and commercial photography, and their accomplishments were likely superior to American ones.

In early October 2018, Kay and I made a second trip to Tokyo, with a group of eight people on a seventeen-day tour guided by Deaf American expat Peggy Prosser and Deaf Japanese native Meri Hirose. We transported along a mountain sightseeing tour on the twenty-three-mile Takeyama-Kurobe Alpine Route, through seven transportation services using five modes, (funicular, bus, trolleybus, aerial tramway, and walking) along the majestic Japan Alps; and we trekked

Ron and Kay pose in traditional Japanese kimonos in 2018.

along a rugged one-thousand-year-old Nakasendō highway before lodging at a ryōkan. For five hours, we arduously dressed up in kimonos and were professionally photographed at the Warplus Kimono Shop in Nara.

I spoke in ASL with a PowerPoint presentation, with a Japanese Sign Language (JSL) interpreter and a voice interpreter, to a Deaf audience of forty in Tokyo. I was then interviewed by a Deaf TV host, Akira Morita, for the NHK national television network, the American equivalent of ABC, CBS and NBC; Akira is also the vice-principal of the Meisei Gakuen School for the Deaf in Tokyo, a sixty-student private school established in 2008 that provides bilingual/bicultural education in JSL.

NORWAY

In the spring of 1997, Kay and I attended the now-closed Norway Fair at Fort Mason in San Francisco. We browsed an exhibition presented by Norwegian Coastal Voyages and gathered brochures. We immediately made a reservation and selected a coastal ferry date close to the summer solstice. After spending a few days in Oslo, we rode a train towards Bergen. About halfway, we transferred to a bus, then a fjord cruise, and then another bus to the next train station.

Upon arriving, we had to drag our luggage through cobbled streets for a few blocks to our hotel overlooking a fish market and a harbor. After a day of touring, we dined at a nearby restaurant and met a small group of Deaf people who gathered there each month.

In the early evening, we rode by taxi from the harbor across the hill to the opposite harbor to an awaiting ferry. After embarking, we told the receptionist that we were Deaf. She became so flustered that she quickly called a manager; they both looked stunned. Slowly, they awkwardly began to communicate with us. Finally, they guided us to a reserved starboard cabin so we could observe the coast as well as embarking and disembarking passengers, cars, trucks, and cargoes at each port.

Kay and I found ourselves the only Americans on the ferry; all other passengers were Europeans. We asked English-speaking people from Great Britain and South Africa for assistance with the spoken information and they willingly shared the information. We were the only passengers who disembarked at the Lapland town of Kirkenes at the northernmost end of Norway. From there, we flew back to Oslo and then to Copenhagen for the opening of the Deaflympics.

SWITZERLAND

Switzerland officially has four regional languages, and is comprised of 63 percent German, 23 percent French, 8 percent Italian and 1 percent Romansh people. The respective sign languages are Swiss-German Sign Language (DSGS), French Sign Language (LSF), and Italian Sign Language (LIS).

In 1985, Christian "Cricri" Gremaud visited us in San Francisco as a teenager. In July 2001, Kay and I flew to Switzerland to visit him. We stayed at his five-member family's cozy two-story residence in Maly, a village three miles south of the bilingual city of Fribourg or Freiburg, established in 1157.

His amicable father Gérard was a renowned university physics professor at the Swiss Federal Institute of Technology in Lausanne. Gérard also authored textbooks and was a lecturer at international conferences, and enjoyed gourmet cooking using wine from his cellar. As a retiree, he tinkered with electricity and electronics around the house.

One evening, Cricri invited us to dine with a large group of Deaf people at a smoke-filled restaurant in Fribourg. He introduced us to everyone, including Christian Doussé and Florence Guillet, who we had once met at Gallaudet in 1997. After dinner, Florence's friend Christophe Hasenfratz from Zurich playfully and drunkly piled dirty dishes on the table so high that Christian stopped him.

Accompanied by Cricri, we flew down to Rome for the Deaflympics on July 22-August 1. The games were so chaotic that we decided to sightsee in the ancient city instead. Even though Cricri had never been there, we were amazed by what a great tour guide he was, all because he had done research.

After attending a papal audience with Pope John Paul II at the Vatican, Cricri received a shocking mobile message from his father about the murder-suicide of Florence and Christophe, the same people we had met in Fribourg, and another friend from Kenya. We later learned that while studying at Gallaudet the Kenyan, who also worked part-time for security on campus, had taught Florence English, which was required for enrollment. One evening, the Kenyan and Florence dined with Christophe and Christian at a restaurant in nearby Gruyères. Christophe drove Florence and the Kenyan back to her apartment in Fribourg while Christian went home alone. Between 11:00 p.m. and midnight, Christophe shot the Kenyan dead and seriously wounded Florence; she died in the ambulance en route to the hospital. Christophe escaped and then committed suicide. In 2017, I researched that tragedy at the Gallaudet archives, but found nothing. It was odd that nobody on campus was aware of that crime.

Cricri was a graduate of the University of Fribourg and was an LSF reporter in Switzerland and France, also hosting an LSF program for a television station in Geneva. He also served as a consultant for a Deaf non-profit organization in Berne. Today, CriCri is a communication and marketing leader at the Swiss Federation of the Deaf in Zurich. He can converse in eight sign languages and writes and reads in four languages.

RUSSIA

Ron and Kay in front of the
St. Basil Cathedral in Moscow.

Vladmir Galchenko was
a Deaf Russian who designed
a space shuttle.

During the summer of 2010, seventeen of us visited post-Soviet Russia. In Moscow, our Deaf guide was Victor Palenny, who used ASL. Possessing a doctorate degree in methodology, he authored five books in Russian: three on Deaf history, one on Deaf artists, and one manual about being Deaf for hearing audiologists and doctors. He also was an active leader in sports competitions such as the Deaflympics.

We were completely floored during our visit to the museum at a Deaf club, seeing a giant poster featuring Vladimir Galchenko (1937-2003), who was Deaf and the leading designer of a space shuttle. In 1994, the Gallaudet University Alumni Association awarded its Amos Kendall

Award to Vladmir in recognition of his notable excellence in a professional field not related to being Deaf. There also was a bust designed by a Deaf sculptor that depicted Konstantin Tsiolkovsky (1867-1935), a Deaf man who is considered the father of space travel theory used by many scientists and physicists today. In fact, a crater on the far side of the moon is named after Konstantin.

We toured Saint Petersburg, led by a Deaf ASL signing guide Nikolay Suslov, who instructs art classes at a Deaf school in Pavlovsk. In 1807, the school was the first Russian Deaf school, established by Dowager Empress Maria Feodorovna after she met a Deaf boy. It consists of a trade school and a college. Nikolay's English was so impeccable that it exceeded my fluency. He and his wife once worked at a fish cannery in Alaska. We maintain contact to this day.

CUBA

During the early months of the 1959 revolution led by Fidel Castro and Ernesto "Che" Guevara, Deaf Cuban people were deprived of their human rights and replaced at their places of employment.

Kay, at far left, enjoys drinks with Deaf Cuban guides Angela Fer and Lourdes Garcia.

In January 2019, Kay and I flew to Cuba. A Deaf local guide, Angela Fer, who signed in ASL and Cuban Sign Language (LSC) worked along with a hard of hearing interpreter, Lourdes Garcia, who spoke in Spanish as fluently as she signed in LSC. There was another couple with us from New York. Unlike luxury hotels and cruises we had stayed at in the past, we stayed at small, humble hostels that served savory home-cooked meals and provided comfortable beds with thick foam mattresses. We observed local people and their daily routines. In rural areas, people used horses for local transportation and farming because they couldn't afford cars nor tractors. The rural freeways were full of potholes. Socialist propaganda signs were posted everywhere.

Sadly, Deaf Cubans have been extremely discriminated against. Unlike their hearing peers, they do not receive monthly public benefits from the Communist government. However, they are admitted free at hospitals whenever sick or injured. Even so, Deaf Cubans are forced to perform odd jobs to make ends meet. In contrast, the Soviet Union helped Deaf Russians by subsidizing Deaf towns, Deaf factories, Deaf clubs, and Deaf housing until its collapse in 1989.

Ron and Kay stand in front of a skyscraper in Taipei, Taiwan in 2009.

Kay at an Ukrainian Deaf Society exhibit in Kyiv in 2010.

Ron (in bed) and Kay (second from right) pose in a tradtional Ryokan bedroom with their travel group in 2018.

Ron and Kay at El Nido in Palawan, Philippines in 2017.

Ron and Kay at the Morro Castle in Havana, Cuba in 2019.

TIMELINE

1800s	1871	Grandfather Hanakichi Hirano is born in Japan.
	1874	Grandmother Ina Watanabe is born in Sendai in Miyagi Prefecture.
	1882	Grandfather George Shiro Morioka is born in Hiroshima Prefecture.
	1887	Grandmother Fuji Hata is born in Yokohama in Kanagawa Prefecture.
1900s	1902	Hanakichi Hirano and Ina Watanabe marry in Japan.
	1903	James Hirano is born in Nagano Prefecture.
	1906	George Shiro Morioka comes to San Francisco from Hawaii.
	1908	George Shiro Morioka and Fuji Hata marry in San Francisco.
	1909	Mary Morioka is born in San Francisco. Hanakichi, Ina, and James Hirano immigrate to Oakland.
1910s		
1920s	1920	Grandfather Hanakichi dies at the age of 49.
1930s	1932	James Hirano and Mary Morioka are married in Oakland, California. Ron Hirano is born in Berkeley.
	1938	Ron enrolls at the California School for the Deaf in Berkeley.
1940s	1942	The Hirano and Morioka families are incarcerated in internment camps. Delight Rice takes over the guardianship of Ron, and he continues his education at CSD.
	1945	Grandfather Shiro dies at the age of 63.

1950s	1952	Ron graduates from CSD and begins attending Gallaudet College in Washington, DC.
	1955	Ron earns the college's first associate of arts degree, and is awarded his degree at the very same commencement where Delight Rice is conferred with an honorary doctorate.
	1956	Ron becomes a founding president of the Guys and Gals Club in San Francisco.
	1957	Ron starts full-time employment as a draftsperson at Metalco in Emeryville, California.
	1958	Grandmother Fuji dies at the age of 71. Ron becomes a junior draftsperson at Soulé Steel Company in San Francisco.
1960s	1960	Ron first meets and begins dating Catherine "Kay" Farkas.
	1962	Ron and Kay marry in Milwaukee, WI.
	1964	Delight Rice dies at the age of 81.
	1966	Ron becomes a leader and alpine guide for backpacking and mountaineering treks along the High Sierra.
1970s	1971	Ron and Kay purchase their first home in San Francisco.
	1972	Ron becomes the chairperson of the CSD Class of 1952's twentieth anniversary reunion in Berkeley.
	1974	Ron is a project manager at Gavin Company in San Leandro, California.
	1977	Ron becomes a part-time instructor at Ohlone College in Fremont, California. He also chairs the CSD Class of 1952's twenty-fifth anniversary reunion in Fremont, CA.
1980s	1980	Grandmother Ina dies at the age of 106.
	1982	Ron is an instructor of drafting and design technology at SouthWest Collegiate Institute for the Deaf in Big Spring, Texas. His father James dies at the age of 80.

| 1984 | Ron obtains a bachelor's degree from San Francisco State University after one year of study. |

| 1985 | He is appointed as a family trustee by his mother. He also becomes the owner of The Tax Signs, an income tax service, while being employed as a draftsman and engineer at Blakeway Metal Works in San Francisco. |

1990s | 1993 | Ron becomes a draftsperson at Forderer Cornice Works in San Francisco. |

| 1994 | He serves as board treasurer of Deaf Counseling, Advocacy & Referral Agency. |

| 1995 | Ron retires at the age of 63. |

| 1996 | He is elected as the founding treasurer of the Bay Area Coalition of Deaf Senior Citizens (BACDSC). |

| 1997 | Ron is elected as board treasurer of the Deaf Seniors of America (DSA). |

| 1999 | Ron becomes the board president of DEAF Media. |

2000s | 2000 | Ron's mother Mary dies at the age of 91. |

| 2002 | Ron is elected as the second vice-president of BACDSC, and serves as the editor of the CSD Class of 1952 newsletter. He also chairs the Class of 1952's fiftieth anniversary reunion. |

| 2004 | Ron becomes editor of the BACDSC newsletter. |

| 2005 | He successfully chairs the DSA national conference in San Francisco. |

| 2006 | Ron is elected as BACDSC president. |

| 2007 | Ron gives a tribute speech in honor of Delight Rice's founding of the Philippine School for the Deaf at its centennial celebration. |

| 2009 | He is elected as the board vice-president of CSD Alumni Association, and serves as editor of the CSDAA newsletter. |

2010s | 2010 | He is inducted into the CSD Heritage Hall of Fame-Community in Fremont. |

2014 Ron authors his first book, *The Life Story of Mother Delight Rice and Her Children*. He presents at public libraries in Washington, DC and San Francisco.

2015 Ron presents at Ohlone College in Fremont, and travels to the Philippines with his wife for a book tour.

2017 Ron authors and publishes a second book, *Gallaudet University Class of 1957 60th Anniversary Edition*, distributed exclusively to the forty-nine surviving classmates. He and Kay also unveil a statue of Delight Rice at the Philippine School for the Deaf.

2018 Ron continues to present about the book around the country and in Japan. He is inducted into the Deaf American Distance Running Hall of Fame. He also is interviewed about the incarceration camps for the national NHK television station in Tokyo.

2020s

2020 After watching a videotaped 1993 interview with his mother, Ron resumes revising his autobiography and begins to prepare it for publication amidst the pandemic.

2021 Ron's autobiography is published.

APPENDIX A
COMMUNITY SERVICE

BAY AREA ASIAN DEAF ASSOCIATION
- **1994**: Advisor for 1994 San Francisco Access Silent Asia Conference (First national conference on Asian Deaf) committee
- **2006-2007**: Advisor for 2007 San Francisco National Asian Deaf Congress committee
- **2014**: Advisor for 2014 Berkeley National Asian Deaf Congress committee

BAY AREA COALITION OF DEAF SENIOR CITIZENS
- **1996-2002**: Founding board treasurer
- **1999-2005**: Chairperson of San Francisco 2005 DSA Conference committee
- **2002-2006**: Board second vice-president
- **2004-2010**: Editor of *Senior Quest* newsletter
- **2006-2010**: Board president

CALIFORNIA SCHOOL FOR THE DEAF ALUMNI ASSOCIATION
- **2009-2015**: Board vice-president
- **2009-2010**: Editor of *The Alumni Eagle* newsletter

CALIFORNIA SCHOOL FOR THE DEAF
CLASS OF 1952
- **1972**: Chairperson of 20th anniversary reunion in Berkeley
- **1977**: Chairperson of 25th anniversary reunion in Fremont

- **2000-2003**: Editor of *1952 Eagles* newsletter
- **2002**: Chairperson of 50th anniversary reunion in San Francisco

DEAF COUNSELING, ADVOCACY & REFERRAL AGENCY
- **1977-1979**: Board member under President Michael Finneran
- **1992-1994**: Board member under President Ronald Rhodes
- **1994-1999**: Board treasurer under President Diana Herron

DEAF MEDIA
1999-2001: Board president

DEAF SENIORS OF AMERICA
1997-2003: Board treasurer

GALLAUDET UNIVERSITY ALUMNI ASSOCIATION
2007: Member of nomination screening committee

GUYS AND GALS CLUB
1956-1958: Founder and president

PHILIPPINE SCHOOL FOR THE DEAF CENTENNIAL COMMITTEE
2006-2007: Treasurer of Filipino-American fundraising committee

APPENDIX B
AWARDS & HONORS

1994
- Appreciation Award by Deaf Counseling, Advocacy & Referral Agency (DCARA)

2000
- Hal Ramger Distinguished Service Award by DCARA
- Certificate of Appreciation by DCARA

2001
- Certificate of Appreciation by DEAF Media

2003
- Certificate of Appreciation by Deaf Seniors of America
- Distinguished Service Award by Deaf Seniors of America

2005
- Award by Bay Area Coalition of Deaf Senior Citizens

2007
- Distinguished Service Award by California Association of the Deaf
- Certificate of Appreciation by National Asian Deaf Congress
- Plaque of Appreciation by Philippine School for the Deaf Centennial Committee

2009
- Executive Director's Award by DCARA
- Pauline "Polly" Peikoff "Service to Others" Award by Gallaudet University Alumni Association

2010
- Senior Citizens Award by National Association of the Deaf
- California School for the Deaf Heritage Hall of Fame for Community

2014

- Trailblazer Award by DCARA

2015

- Certificate of Appreciation by Republic of the Philippines Department of Education and Philippine School for the Deaf
- Certificate of Appreciation by De La Salle-College of Saint Benilde School of Deaf Education and Applied Studies
- Certificate of Appreciation by De La Salle-College of Saint Benilde School of Deaf Education and Applied Studies
- Hal Ramger Distinguished Service Award by DCARA

2017

- Plaque of Appreciation by Philippine School for the Deaf Alumni Affairs Association

Ron poses with an award given by Deaf Seniors of America in 2003.

2018

- Induction in Deaf American Distance Running Hall of Fame Inaugural Class of 2018

2019

- Plaque of Appreciation by Gallaudet Class of 1957

AFTERWORD

I originally planned to write this book right after I finished my first book in 2015, *The Life Story of Mother Delight Rice and Her Children*, but it was delayed for three years due to a family controversy.

During that hiatus, I authored, designed, and published the unprecedented Gallaudet University Class of 1957 sixtieth anniversary book. In October 2017, copies were distributed to the surviving forty-nine (of ninety-six) classmates. The book concludes with one of my mottoes, "Who is your boss? Your body, not your head."

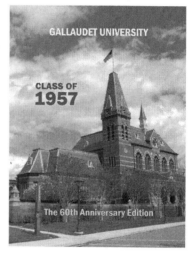

After the family controversy settled down, I resumed writing this book in the spring of 2018. In early January 2020, my brother Daniel emailed me his 1993 videotaped interview of our late mother, eleven hours long, so I had to rewrite the book. Later in the same month, Daniel dispatched me a two-hour videotaped interview Lu Ann Sleeper conducted with me at the University of California in Berkeley in 2013. That meant more revisions.

In the United States and the Philippines, people at my presentations on my first book often asked me about my background. As I am the eldest of six siblings, my younger siblings and their children are also curious about my early life. Thus, this book was written.

On November 28, 2020, I celebrated my 88th birthday, and celebrated it virtually via Facebook given the pandemic. In Japanese culture, *Beiju* (米寿) is known as the long-life celebration milestone that deserves a special celebration, also known as *yone no iwai*. This popularity came about because the Japanese character for the number 88 resembles the character of rice when written together; rice, when translated to Japanese, is *bei*.

I received an outpouring of love from friends about my birthday. They meant so much to me that I want to share a few excerpts.

Febe Sevilla: Happy Quarantine birthday, Ron. Thank you for writing the biggest and most important chunk of [Filipino Deaf] history of Filipino, the life story of Delight Rice. Mother Delight is surely proud of what you've accomplished. Her statue. . . is now silently looking at all the deaf students coming in and out of PSD. . .[a] testament to the love and gratitude of countless deaf and blind students whose lives she touched and greatly improved. We are forever grateful for all your hard work.

Alice L. Hagemeyer: Happy 88th birthday to my best friend, Ronald Hirano, since our Gallaudet years. The best of the Class of 1957, for his words of wisdom about the values of sharing stories!!! Already the author of two books and more to come.

Peggy L. Prosser: Beautiful! You're one of the most amazing Deaf people I've met. I feel lucky to have gotten to know you. You're more than history, you're a person of character. And I have my highest respect for you. Happy Birthday.

Ellen Thielman: Happy Birthday Ron! Glad I got to know you while we traveled to Japan and I thought, "Wow, what a fun character to travel with," and you made us laugh with your humor and wit.

For most of my life, I have spent time reading, reading, and reading. As my sister Janet said in the foreword, my head was always buried in a book even during family dinners. As a result, I have experienced enriching years as writer, editor and designer of newsletters and books. I hope you have enjoyed this book while I continue my travels, hobbies, and love of life.

Deaf people can do anything hearing people can, except hear.

— Frederick Schreiber
First executive director of the
National Association of the Deaf